THE GREAT LIVES SERIES

Great Lives biographies shed an exciting new light on the many dynamic men and women whose actions, visions, and dedication to an ideal have influenced the course of history. Their ambitions, dreams, successes and failures, the controversies they faced and the obstacles they overcame are the true stories behind these distinguished world leaders, explorers, and great Americans.

Other biographies in the Great Lives Series

CHRISTOPHER COLUMBUS: The Intrepid Mariner

MIKHAIL GORBACHEV: The Soviet Innovator

JOHN F. KENNEDY: Courage in Crisis

ABRAHAM LINCOLN: The Freedom President

SALLY RIDE: Shooting for the Stars

ACKNOWLEDGMENT

A special thanks to educators Dr. Frank Moretti, Ph.D., Associate Headmaster of the Dalton School in New York City; Dr. Paul Mattingly, Ph.D., Professor of History at New York University; and Barbara Smith, M. S., Assistant Superintendent of the Los Angeles Unified School District, for their contributions to the Great Lives Series.

GREAT LIVES

HARRIET TUBMAN
CALL TO FREEDOM

Judy Carlson

FAWCETT COLUMBINE
NEW YORK

For middle school readers

A Fawcett Columbine Book
Published by Ballantine Books

Library of Congress Catalogue Card Number: 89-90818

ISBN: 0-449-90376-1

Cover design and illustration by Paul Davis

Manufactured in the United States of America

First Edition: September 1989

20 19 18 17 16 15 14 13 12 11

TABLE OF CONTENTS

Harriet Tubman was a woman of faith and action. As a "conductor" on the Underground Railroad, she guided runaway slaves from the South to freedom in the North. This woodcut dates from the Civil War, when she served as a scout, spy, and nurse. For her lifetime of work in perilous situations, Harriet Tubman came to be known as the Moses of her people.

1

Flight to Freedom!

HARRIET WAS RUNNING.
The moon shed a faint light, just enough so Harriet could see a few yards in front of her, but she had no path or road to guide her. The woods she was running through were overgrown with bushes, brambles, and trees. The land was unfamiliar; she had left the forests she knew so well only hours before. She only knew that she wanted to head north, and the North Star shining faintly above in the black sky pointed the way.

Harriet Tubman, a fugitive slave, was running for her life, and yet, strangely enough, she was not afraid. Her heart was pounding because she was running, not because of fear. Her eyes strained to see ahead, but she heard only her own footsteps, the sound of her breathing, and the occasional animal she frightened as she plunged through the trees. Still, she had never in her life listened so hard for

1

other sounds: the barking of pursuing dogs, the hoofbeat of slave catcher's horses, the voices of slave hunters who might be on her trail.

"Keep movin,' " Harriet told herself. As she stumbled over fallen branches, sharp brambles tore at her clothes, but Harriet didn't care.

"I'm gon' be free," she thought to herself. Harriet knew she could make it because she was strong — stronger than most men. She'd run forever if she had to. She'd eat wild plants and berries to stay alive. "I've endured the whip, I've endured beatings, I've endured slavery," she said to herself. "I can endure anything now in order to be free."

As Harriet ran through the dark woods of Dorchester County, Maryland, that night in 1849, thoughts of the life she was leaving flashed through her mind: her husband, a free black man; her parents, both still slaves; her seven brothers and sisters, slaves, too, and the two lost sisters sold south; the cruel overseer whom Harriet and the other slaves hated. She wouldn't miss the backbreaking work from sunup to sundown or the whippings that made her back bleed. Harriet was leaving behind more than twenty years — her whole life — of slavery!

What if she was caught? Harriet wouldn't think about it. "Keep runnin'," she told herself. "No one can catch you. The Lord is runnin' with you." Every slave knew what happened to runaways who were caught. They were whipped to within an inch of their lives, and then they usually were sold into a chain gang heading to the Deep South, where conditions for slaves were far worse even than here in Maryland.

She talked to God as she ran. "Oh, dear Lord, I haint got no friend but you," she said. "Come to my help, Lord, for I'm in trouble!"

Harriet was getting tired now. The sky was getting lighter and the birds broke into song. Dawn was near and the woods were waking up. She had been running all night.

Harriet's mind went back two nights to her first attempt at escape. That night she had convinced two of her brothers to come with her. She had heard rumors they were all to be sold soon. Together they had started out, but in the dark woods her brothers' fears and apprehensions grew.

"When morning comes, they're gon' set the dogs out after us," they said to Harriet. "Those dogs are awful mean. They can rip a man apart."

"They won't sniff us out," Harriet said, her voice steady. "We'll wade through streams, they'll lose the scent."

But more doubts crept into her brothers' minds. Their master would call out a search party. Posters with their names and descriptions would be spread throughout the region. Everyone would be looking for them. Who would help three poor slaves? How could they ever hope to make it to a free state in the North when they had no money and no connections? They had no map to guide them, and couldn't even have read one. Like most slaves, neither Harriet nor her brothers knew how to read or write.

3

"We're going back," her brothers had said at last. "We go back now, we'll make it by morning. No one will know we was gone."

Harriet had shaken her head sadly. This escape had been her idea. She had planned it and she was going to follow through with it. She wanted her brothers to be free with her, but if they wanted to go back, she was helpless to stop them. She turned back with them. But Harriet knew that she could be a slave no longer. Two nights later, she ran away on her own.

"There are two things I have a right to, liberty or death," she later declared. "If I can't have one, I will have the other. For no man will take me alive. I will fight for my liberty as long as my strength lasts, and when the time comes for me to go, the Lord will let them take me."

Now, as the sun came up, Harriet moved cautiously. By now she must be close to the house where she might find refuge from the slave catchers. In her pocket was her ticket to freedom: a slip of paper with the name of someone who would help her. She couldn't read the name. All she knew was that this was someone ready to risk sheltering a runaway slave.

As Harriet slowed down her run and unfolded the paper, she remembered the day she was given it. Harriet had been working in the fields, when a white woman who was of the Quaker faith had talked to her. Harriet, like most slaves, knew that Quakers were fierce abolitionists, that is, they were adamant that slavery was evil and should be abolished.

"If you ever need help," the woman told her when they talked, "come to me." So while on an errand for her master, Harriet had stopped by the Quaker woman's home.

"I need help," Harriet said in a low voice. The Quaker woman looked at her closely. She knew what Harriet meant.

"Here," she said, and she wrote down a name and gave Harriet careful directions. "If you're headed north, they'll help you. They're part of the Underground Railroad."

From her childhood, Harriet had heard this phrase. At first she thought it was an actual railroad system built under the ground to carry slaves safely to the free North. Her parents and the other slaves would talk about it in hushed tones at night in their cabins after all the work had been done. Such talk was extremely dangerous and they could not risk the master or the overseer overhearing them. But there was joy and triumph in their voices when they whispered about the slaves who had made it to freedom on the Railroad. These stories gave Harriet and her fellow slaves hope.

Later Harriet found out that the Underground Railroad was not a train system at all, but rather a secret network of people who hated slavery and had organized themselves to help slaves escape. At first they had no name, but one time a slave named Tice Davids crossed the Ohio River in an escape attempt. His master was pursuing close behind, keeping a close eye on Davids as he swam across the river. But on the other side, Davids simply disappeared! When his master could find no trace of him, at last he exclaimed, "He must have gone off on an underground road!" So the escape routes north came to be called the Underground Railroad.

Harriet never tired of hearing that story and all the other Underground Railroad stories. She was awed at the daring and resourcefulness of the escaping slaves. She was amazed that some white folk would risk their lives to help black slaves. These people had made their homes and barns into hiding places which were called "stations." Slaves would hide in a station until a "conductor" could transport them to the next stop. Some slaves traveled in wagons, hidden beneath blankets, boards, or produce, while others went disguised on steamboats or trains. Still others traveled by foot in the black of night from station to station. Their goal was to make it to one of the eighteen free states. Their goal was to be a slave no longer!

Now Harriet herself was about to board the Underground Railroad. She didn't care if it was a real train system or not; she just wanted that ride to freedom. Harriet stood at the edge of the forest and saw before her a cluster of tidy little houses. The Quaker woman had described the first safe place where Harriet should find shelter on her journey north. Now, as the sun came up, she hoped she would find it. One house matched the description, so Harriet moved toward it.

Her body was exhausted from her all-night journey, but as she opened the gate and went in the yard, her mind and emotions were churning. What if this was the wrong house? What if the people had moved? What if they would betray her? She paused before knocking and tried to calm her mind. She quickly brushed off some of the dirt and brambles clinging to her dress and knocked on the door. A white woman answered. Harriet thrust the slip of paper into the woman's hand.

"A friend said you could help me," Harriet said nervously.

The woman looked around the yard. "Here, take this broom," the woman softly told Harriet. "Sweep the yard." Harriet looked confused. Didn't this woman know what she wanted?

"Our neighbors," the woman said in a low voice, "they might see. If you rested now, they might think it suspicious. This way they'll think we hired you to work." Harriet took the broom and swept. Only after she had worked awhile did the white woman come and call her to come in.

Inside, she brought Harriet food and drink. Then she took Harriet to a room where she could rest her weary muscles and sleep. That evening, the woman's husband hid Harriet in his wagon and drove her to the edge of town.

"Head that way," he told her, pointing to a footpath off the road. He described the next place she could stop.

Harriet gratefully thanked him. Once again, she set off through unknown territory for an unknown home and unknown "hosts." She was on the Underground Railroad now. Naturally, she could not travel on the road where she could be seen, so Harriet had to pick her way through brambles and underbrush, climb over fallen trees, and wade through rushing streams. By night she went by the North Star. All of the slaves knew about the North Star.

"Keep your eyes on it," Harriet's father told her as a child. "It'll lead you to freedom." On cloudy nights the North Star could not be seen, but Harriet's father, who worked as a slave cutting and hauling timber in the forest, had taught her how to survive in the wilds. She knew what plants to eat, and which could be used for medicines. She also knew that moss always grew on the north side of a tree. So now, when clouds covered the stars at night, she felt for the moss to find her way.

Harriet lost count of the days. Sometimes she found people who gave her food and drink, but often her bed was only the cold ground. As the mists swirled in from the Chesapeake Bay, she felt as though an invisible pillar of cloud by day and of fire by night protected her from danger. She talked to God and seemed to hear him answer. Harriet was sure he was guiding her to freedom, and so she had not an ounce of fear — even though she didn't know how close the slave patrols might be behind her. Sometimes she even sang — snatches of the hymns and spirituals that she loved, and especially her favorite one:

Hail, oh hail, ye happy spirits,
Death no more shall make you fear,
Grief nor sorrow, pain nor anguish,
Shall no more distress you there.

Around Him are ten thousand angels,
Always ready to obey command;
They are always hovering round you,
Till you reach the heavenly land.

Jesus, Jesus will go with you,
He will lead you to his throne;
He who died, has gone before you,
Trod the wine-press all alone.

He whose thunders shake creation,
He who bids the planets roll;
He who rides upon the tempest,
And whose scepter sways the whole.

Dark and thorny is the pathway,
Where the pilgrim makes his ways;
But beyond this vale of sorrow,
Lie the fields of endless days.

Days later, Harriet had traveled well over nine-ty miles as a fugitive. At last she came to the city of Wilmington, Delaware, to the home of Thomas Garrett, a Quaker who ran a shoe store. After allowing Harriet a day to rest and giving her a pair of shoes to replace her worn-out ones, Garrett hid her in his wagon and drove her to the edge of town.

"Keep out of sight," Garrett told Harriet. "These roads are watched constantly since they lead to free states. Use the roads as a guide. Walk until thou seest a wooden sign. This marks the division between states."

Harriet thanked this kind and generous man and set out on her way. Could it be, she wondered, that freedom was less than a day away? Were her years as a slave finally over?

For some time now, the same dream had come to her over and over when she slept. She was flying over fields and towns, rivers and mountains, looking down like a bird. In her dream she finally reached either a great fence or a river, and she tried to fly over it. "But it 'peared," she said, "like I wouldn't have the strength. And just as I was sinkin' down, there would be ladies all dressed in white over there, and they would put out their arms and pull me 'cross."

No longer were Harriet's muscles aching, no more did her bruised and worn feet hurt. When she finally saw the wooden sign that marked the border of Pennsylvania, her heart beat wildly. After a lifetime of being a slave, she was free! She wanted to shout, cry, and sing Alleluias.

Harriet looked at her hands to see if she was the same person. "There was such a glory over everything," she said later. "The sun came like gold through the trees and over the fields, and I felt like I was in Heaven."

Singing, Harriet walked the remaining miles to Philadelphia, where she planned to find work and to live. Harriet Tubman had become a woman of action and a woman of faith.

2

Growing Up a Slave

WHEN HARRIET WAS six years old, her master decided she was old enough to go to work. Edward Brodas of Bucktown, Maryland, was having financial difficulties with his plantation and was selling off one slave after another in order to pay his bills. He was also making money by hiring out some of his slaves for a period of time. Master Edward hired little Harriet out to a white couple, Mr. and Mrs. James Cook. Mrs. Cook was a weaver and Mr. Cook was a trapper. They were not well off, but they decided they could afford a small amount to hire a slave to help them. Of course, they were given the least valuable slave for their money — Harriet.

Mrs. Cook looked doubtfully at Harriet. She was small, even for a six-year-old. She wasn't pretty, didn't appear very bright, and was sullen and slow. In fact, Harriet was terrified at leaving home. She had never been away from her family, much less been expected to work for her living.

At first, Harriet was told she had to help Mrs. Cook with her weaving, but Mrs. Cook was impatient, and Harriet, who was used to playing, did not catch on quickly to what she had to do. Nor did she want to catch on — she wanted to go home.

The Cooks did nothing to make her life pleasant. Harriet had to sleep on the floor in the kitchen and was fed food scraps. When Harriet proved hopeless in helping inside, the Cooks made her work outside. Mr. Cook lined animal traps close to a river that flowed past the house, and it was Harriet's job to wade in the icy cold water to see if the traps had caught any muskrats. Even though Harriet was often freezing, at least she savored the times when she was outdoors and was not forced to be cooped up in the cramped house.

One day she woke up feeling hot and shivery and dizzy — her body covered in red spots. "You're not really sick," the Cooks scoffed. "Come on — get out to work!" Though Harriet felt too weak to stand, she had to obey, and in the bitter cold she stumbled out to the water to check the lines. Feeling worse and worse, she finally staggered back into the house and collapsed. Mr. Cook and his wife looked at Harriet, lying trembling and moaning on her blanket in the kitchen. "What are we going to do with her now?" Mr. Cook asked as he looked at the pitiful child.

"She's been nothing but trouble," Mrs. Cook grumbled. "She hasn't been worth the few cents we've paid for her."

"But what should we do?" Mr. Cook asked. "She may die! She looks bad. What if she dies?" Harriet moaned and tossed in her bed. Mrs. Cook frowned as she looked at her unsympathetically.

"We'd better take her back right away," she said with a scowl. "If she dies on us, Brodas will probably want us to pay for her. We don't have that kind of money." The Cooks tossed an old blanket over Harriet and drove her back to Master Edward's plantation.

Harriet's mother, Old Rit, could scarcely believe her eyes when they brought Harriet into her cabin. Her little girl was filthy, terribly thin, and feverish.

"She has the measles!" Old Rit exclaimed after she examined the ill child. Harriet, sick and weak, looked up at her mother gratefully — she was home at last. Slowly Old Rit nursed her young daughter back to health, and though she recovered, after that illness Harriet's voice always sounded husky and low.

This episode with the Cooks was Harriet's first personal experience of the horror of slavery. But her family had been suffering under it ever since Harriet's grandmother had been kidnapped from her village in Africa and sold into slavery in America many years before.

Like many other kidnapped blacks, she was brought to the United States to work as slave labor on Southern plantations. Harriet was of pure African heritage on her mother and father's side. She later told friends that she was descended from

A cotton plantation on the Mississippi River. Living conditions for slaves on Southern plantations were harsh, to say the least. They worked from sunrise to sundown, had little to eat, and were frequently beaten for minor offenses.

the Ashanti, a rebellious and courageous African people.

Slavery had existed in the United States ever since the early 1500s. Historians estimate that between 15 million and 100 million Africans were brought to North America, most of them sold to Southerners who wanted cheap labor to make a profit on their tobacco and cotton crops. Northerners, who didn't rely solely on crops to earn their living, were against or indifferent to slavery.

Because Harriet's grandmother was forced into slavery, her children and their children automatically became slaves, too. When Harriet grew up, and was still a slave, she paid a lawyer five dollars to look up the will of her mother's first master. He told her that her mother should have been freed when that master's granddaughter died. No one ever told Harriet's mother this. So even though Rit was still young when the granddaughter died, she was never freed. She remained a slave and all of her children were born into slavery.

Harriet was born in a one-room cabin in 1820 or 1821 — she was never quite sure which. No records were kept of slave births. Her parents were Ben Ross and Harriet (Old Rit) Greene, but she belonged to Master Edward. Her parents named her Araminta, but when she got older people called her by her mother's name, Harriet. Harriet's parents were hard-working and smart — valuable slaves to Master Edward. Ben worked in the fields and in the woods, and was often put in charge of other slaves while Old Rit labored in the fields. Both parents were proud of Harriet, the youngest of their ten children.

The night Harriet was born a slave, Old Rit cradled her baby daughter in her arms. She wished that her child would have an easier life than she had had. "Perhaps you'll work in the Big House," she whispered to her daughter. The Big House was what the slaves called their master's large dwelling. Old Rit didn't want her daughter to have to toil from dawn to dusk under the hot sun, lashed by the whip of the overseer as though she were a horse or ox and not a human being.

Old Rit didn't get a chance to spend a lot of time with her new baby because, like most slave mothers, she was only allowed two weeks to a month to stay home and care for her newborn. Then she was back at work picking cotton and tobacco in the fields. Baby Harriet and the other slave children, still too small to work, were taken care of by one or two old slave women who were no longer able to toil in the fields. A cabin was set aside for the slave children's nursery, with a fenced-in yard where the young children could crawl or toddle around. In most cases, Harriet and the children would eat their meals out of one large pot, eating mostly with their hands, or they would share one spoon between them. Each child would take a spoonful of food and then pass the spoon to the next child.

As Harriet was growing up, she and all the other slave children wore a garment that looked like a long shirt or a big gunnysack. An opening was cut out for the head to go through and two holes were cut for the arms to go through. Boys and girls dressed alike and few slave children wore underclothes. Harriet and the other children had only one such outfit, and they wore it until it wore out. They went barefoot all year round.

Master Edward didn't bother much about the slave children, but if he thought they could bring in some money, he wanted to use them any way he could. So, just as soon as Harriet had recovered from the measles and had regained most of her strength, Master Edward sent her back to the Cooks. Once again they tried unsuccessfully to teach her how to weave, but Harriet hated Mrs. Cook and had no desire to work indoors, so they sent her back.

Master Edward then hired her out again — this time to a Miss Susan. Harriet was supposed to keep the house clean and take care of Miss Susan's little baby. Harriet had been around babies before, but she had never had sole responsibility for one. Nor had she ever been taught how to dust or clean a house. She was to clean all day and attend the baby all night.

"Make sure the baby doesn't cry," Miss Susan told her. "If he cries, you get whipped." The first morning, Miss Susan handed Harriet a dustcloth. "Don't just stand there — get to work," she commanded. "Move these chairs and tables into the middle of the room, sweep the carpet clean, then dust everything, and put them back in their places! I expect this to be clean by the time I return." She put her whip on the mantel as a warning to Harriet.

When she left, Harriet looked at the dustcloth in her hands. The seven-year-old girl had no idea what to do. She had never seen anyone dust, much less tried it herself. There was not too much in her parents' one-room cabin beside the dirt floor, and no one dusted there.

Harriet was frightened, but doing her best, she swept the room with all of her strength. Dust flew — then she wiped the furniture until, as she said, "you could see your face in 'em, they shone so." But the dust quickly settled back down on the furniture. When Miss Susan returned, she saw that the dust was still everywhere.

"You lazy girl!" she yelled. "I wanted it clean in here! You've done nothing!"

"Miss Susan, I swept and dusted just as you told me," Harriet said. Enraged at her slave's impertinence, Miss Susan took the whip down and began beating the little girl on the head, face, and neck.

"Do it right," Miss Susan shrieked, and left.

Harriet, more frightened and confused than before, didn't know what to do. Once again, she ran the dustcloth over the table and chairs. Once again, Miss Susan returned to find dust everywhere, and this time she whipped Harriet even harder. Harriet screamed and pleaded for her to stop, but Miss Susan kept whipping the child until finally her sister, Miss Emily, heard Harriet's cries and came into the room.

"Susan! Stop that!" Miss Emily said. "If you do not stop whipping that child, I will leave your house and never come back!"

"This girl is either lazy or plain stupid!" Miss Susan said in disgust. "She can't even do a simple task like dusting!"

"Did you take the time to teach her?" Miss Emily inquired. And with that, Miss Emily showed Harriet how to open the windows and sweep. When the dust settled on the tables and chairs, she showed her how to wipe it off. And Harriet, who was neither lazy nor stupid, caught on immediately.

Each night, when her long day's work was over, seven-year-old Harriet had to take care of the baby while its mother slept. To get the baby to sleep, she sat and held it in her arms, or rocked it in its cradle. Often she would fall asleep and stop rocking and the baby would cry. At the noise, Miss Susan would get up — not to comfort her child, but to whip Harriet. Harriet was expected to put in a full day's work with little to no sleep — and she was still a small child!

Not only did Harriet have to get by on only a few hours of sleep, but she also had to suffer with a back and neck that were continually covered with the wounds of the whip. In time, life became unbearable for little Harriet.

As she later told a friend, "One morning, after breakfast, Miss Susan had the baby, and I stood by the table waiting until I was to take it. Near me was a bowl of lumps of white sugar . . . . Now you know, I never had anything good, no sweet, no sugar. And that sugar, right by me, did look so nice, and my mistress's back was turned to me while she was fighting with her husband, so I just put my fingers in the sugar bowl to take one lump and maybe she heard me for she turned and saw me."

Incensed, Miss Susan reached for her whip. Harriet, who had been beaten for virtually nothing before, did not need telling that she was now in for the whipping of her life. She took off out the door and ran like the wind.

Miss Susan and her husband chased after her, but Harriet was fast and kept running until she realized she was no longer being followed. But Harriet had no idea where she was or how to get back to her parents, and she knew people would start to look for her soon. Finally she came to a large pigpen that had a sow with a large litter of little pigs.

"And there I stayed from Friday until the next Tuesday, fighting with those little pigs for the potato peelings and other scraps that came down in the trough," she remembered.

At last Harriet grew too hungry, and having nowhere else to go, she returned to Miss Susan's to face her inevitable punishment. Harriet was brutally lashed until her back and neck were bloody. Then Miss Susan, disgusted and angry, returned the starved, hurt girl to Master Brodas. "She's not worth sixpence," was all she said.

Old Rit wept when she saw her daughter brought back in such an abused condition. The child was nothing but skin and bone, and covered with ugly scars and massive bruises. Nevertheless, Old Rit was glad to have her little daughter home. Surely their master would have pity on little Harriet now and let the pitiful child stay with her mother.

No sooner was Harriet back on her feet than her greedy master hired her out again. This time, it was to a man who made her work outside, lifting barrels of flour, loading wagons, hoeing, plowing, and doing other jobs that demanded physical strength. Harriet spent the rest of her childhood at back-breaking work that made her strong — very strong. Because she never had enough to eat, she never grew taller than five feet, but she was as strong as any man. Harriet didn't mind the hard outdoor work because now she was with her family. And she liked being in the open air working side by side with other slaves. She still was whipped whenever she didn't do exactly what her master or overseer thought she should.

The treatment of some slaves was often inhuman. Harriet saw other slaves being whipped, too — sometimes for little or no reason. Slave owners thought of cruel punishments such as pouring salt on the wounds of slaves they'd just whipped, to cause even more pain. Harriet saw even pregnant women beaten. Sometimes holes were dug in the ground for the pregnant women to lay their swollen stomachs in, so they could receive a beating without their unborn child being hurt. If slaves were caught learning to read or write, a heartless master could cut off one of their fingers or brand them on the face so other slave owners would know they were troublemakers.

Harriet knew no one had a right to treat another human being so cruelly. The thought burned in-

side her that everyone deserved to be free . . . that
it was unjust to keep slaves . . . that freedom was
worth any price.

3

Nat Turner's Rebellion

IT WAS A hot, humid August evening, after eleven-year-old Harriet and her family had put in a hard day's work, that they first heard about Nat Turner. They had eaten supper and were sitting outside their cabin talking with their neighbors, when several slaves returned from serving dinner at the Big House.

They huddled together and talked in low voices to the adults, but Harriet could see their excitement. Later, when Harriet's family were in their cabin, Ben told them the news.

"There's a slave in Southampton, Virginia," Ben said, his voice barely audible. "They call him the Prophet. He believes God gave him the mission to deliver our race from bondage. He says he had a vision when God told him to gather up followers and kill the whites — every man, woman and child they come across.

The "discovery" of Nat Turner. Turner was a black slave and preacher who in 1831 led the largest slave revolt in United States history. After his band of fugitive slaves killed sixty whites, it took two months for a Virginia militia to track him down. Though he was promptly sent to the gallows, his defiance brought hope to many Southern slaves.

"Few nights ago, he and six followers killed their master. Then they went from plantation to plantation, killing the white folks and freeing the slaves. Word is that the white folks are organizing to stop them."

Ben went back outside to talk more about it with the other slaves. Harriet lay down on her pallet, but couldn't sleep. What if Nat Turner came and rescued them? Would her father and brothers join the rebellion? Could they really succeed? What would freedom be like? For the first time, freedom seemed really possible to Harriet.

The next day, the slaves went about their work as usual, but they waited eagerly for news. Those slaves who worked in the Big House finally passed the information on to the others. Seventy blacks had joined Nat Turner's army. They were all armed and had killed sixty white people, sparing only those who owned no slaves. The whites sent in the militia to stop them, but it wasn't enough, so they had to call in Federal troops to quell the unrest.

Harriet was jubilant, but next evening she listened to the news in horror. The troops had captured nearly all Turner's followers, and whites in South-ampton had gone on a rampage, slaughtering and torturing blacks, even those who had been loyal. Scores of slaves were dead; fifty-five had been arrested and thrown in jail, but Turner had miraculously escaped.

Where was he? Had he escaped north? Or — Harriet still hoped — maybe he was organizing new troops. Maybe he would still come to rescue her and her family.

The hot summer was over, and still the hunt for Nat Turner continued. All Harriet's daydreams were about him — one day he would certainly reappear, free, armed, and ready to continue the uprising. Harriet was determined she would join him, and though she was small, she thought she was as tough as a grown man.

All kinds of rumors spread quickly throughout the slave's quarters, as well as the Big House. The slaves hoped, and the master dreaded, that Turner was collecting weapons and followers for a new attack. It was late fall when Harriet heard that Nat Turner had been captured. For two months he had hidden in a cave in the wilds, but at last he had been tracked down.

When she heard that Nat Turner refused to plead guilty, and when she heard of his speedy execution, Harriet felt terrible sadness and disappointment, but also pride. Nat Turner had been defeated, but he had not been crushed.

She knew now that the dream of freedom burned in every slave's heart, not just her own. Some slaves had been beaten down so badly they could hardly admit it, even to themselves. But now Harriet had seen that given a chance, freedom was still uppermost in their minds. Slavery was not something people became used to — ever.

The one-room cabin Harriet and her family lived in lay several hundred yards from the master's Big House, along with the other slave cabins. The cabin itself was made of logs that Ben had cut down, with mud and sticks plastered between the logs to hold them together. Mortar was also stuck in the crevices, with hog or cow hair mixed in to make it stick in the cracks. Since the cabin had no windows, the only light came through cracks in the wall or from the rough fireplace. The chimney was made of mud and sticks, which had a dangerous tendency to catch fire. Hanging above the dirt floor near the fireplace were the few pots and pans used for cooking.

Old Rit did most of her cooking in a large three-legged black pot that was called "the spider." All of the food was cooked over the fire — potatoes and corn pone, a kind of corn bread, were roasted in the ashes, and almost everything else boiled in big pots which swung on cranes over the coals. The fireplace also was the only source of heat and light during the cold, dark winters.

Although the cabin was crude, it was home, a place for all of Harriet's family to be together. Harriet loved lying in bed, with her family close by, listening to her parents' low voices talking as she drifted off to sleep. The cabin was crowded with Harriet and her brothers and sisters who hadn't married yet, but she felt safe as long as they were all together.

Being together was something to be valued because most slave owners gave no thought to splitting up black families. Harriet knew it was not unusual for a slave owner to sell a man and not his wife, or children and not their parents. Most owners thought of slaves as being nothing more than property, like the horses that pulled their carriages or the

27

oxen that pulled their plows. A young male slave could be sold for $ 1,500 or more. At a time when a loaf of bread cost pennies, slaves represented a significant investment for the slave owners.

Masters were, of course, all too aware that slaves, unlike animals, could revolt or run away, so the slave owner's goal was to try to keep their slaves subservient by whipping them into submission or by destroying their family units — anything to break their spirit.

Harriet used to say, "It's the way they were brought up. 'Make the little slaves mind you,' they were told, 'or flog them,' is what they said to their children, and they were brought up with the whip in their hands. Now that wasn't the way on all plantations; there were good masters and mistresses, as I've heard tell, but I didn't happen to come across any of them."

Conditions were harsh enough for slaves in Harriet's parents' youth, but after the slave insurrections that occurred during Harriet's childhood, their suffering became even more dreadful. Black codes were developed to keep the slaves in their place — which was as low as a group of people could get. These codes said that slaves had no rights, that they belonged completely to their masters. If slaves tried to escape and were caught, they could be branded on the face with a hot iron or have their ears cropped. If a master whipped a slave to death, the master would not be punished. Slaves could not talk back to their master, and they could not raise a hand to a white person, even in self-defense.

But complete dominion over any group of people is difficult, no matter how severe the restrictions or conditions. Harriet's family and the other slaves found comfort in their strong sense of community. Sunday, the day of rest, was a day when they could meet together and hold informal church services. Here they would hear stories from the Bible and sing songs inspired by them. Often they gathered in the nearby woods late at night to hold their church services in secret, out of the earshot of their white owners. Harriet loved singing, and even though her voice was husky from her bout with measles, it was tuneful and full of feeling. Being with her family and her people, singing the spirituals in rich harmonies, seemed to reach her very soul.

Harriet loved the Bible stories, too, because she and the other slaves could see parallels between their plight and the troubles and sufferings of Biblical characters. Job, for example, suffered terribly as he was afflicted with disease, financial ruin, and family tragedy. Paul was thrown in prison. Noah braved the flood. And Jesus was a particular friend to the slaves because he had suffered just as they were suffering. They turned to Jesus to comfort them and to give them hope.

One song that Harriet loved the most was "Go Down, Moses." In Exodus, Moses and his people, the Israelites, were slaves in a strange land. Just as the black slaves were mistreated by their owners, the Israelite slaves were abused by a Pharaoh. After terrible hardships, Moses led his people to the promised land, to freedom. When Harriet heard this story,

29

she, too, hoped to escape slavery to the land of freedom.

The preacher at these religious meetings was a fellow slave, usually one who could read and write or else who had a good knowledge of the Bible. Harriet and the other slaves would listen to the preacher, then sing and pray, and finally give testimonies about their faith. Though Harriet couldn't read, she knew many Bible passages by heart. In fact, friends later told how Harriet frequently mixed words and phrases from the Bible with her everyday dialect.

Harriet always sang out the spirituals with a passion and a hope.

No fearin', no doubtin'
While God's on our side.
We'll all die we're shoutin'
The Lawd will provide.

Harriet's belief in God played an important role in her life, as was the case with many slaves. The theme of many spirituals was that of faith — faith that everything would work out, faith that a better life would come. Harriet's faith in God gave her hope when she was oppressed, and the confidence to survive the many difficult situations she later faced.

After the Nat Turner uprising, these church services were banned and slaves were even forbidden to read the Bible. Songs like "Go Down, Moses" —

that hinted at rebellion — were prohibited. All the more, Harriet held firmly to her faith.

On weekday evenings, too, after the work was done, the slaves sometimes gathered outside the cabins to talk over the latest news and gossip they had picked up during the day. Slaves who worked in the Big House would overhear news and pass it on to the other slaves. Sometimes they secretly took newspapers and magazines and let a slave who could read tell them what was happening in the world beyond the plantation.

It was under these conditions that Harriet spent her late childhood and adolescence. All these injustices grated against her very soul.

She said, "I think slavery is the next thing to hell. If a person would send another into bondage, he would, it appears to me, be bad enough to send him to hell if he could." But worse times lay ahead of her.

The day the slave traders came was the most horrible in Harriet's life. She ran, with all the other slaves, toward the Big House when she heard about it. Old Rit was standing there with the two babies, Harriet's little niece and nephew. Her other brothers and sisters gathered round — they were screaming and weeping — but Old Rit stood expressionless, stony-faced. The chain gang of slaves was leaving, with two of her sisters.

Harriet's sisters plodded behind the line of slaves, weighed down by the heavy manacles. Harriet ran after them to the edge of the plantation, and watched them trudging down the dusty road. She never saw them again. She never knew what happened to them; suddenly, her two sisters were gone forever.

Harriet knew that her sisters would probably be sold to some master living in the Deep South, so there was no hope of ever seeing or communicating with them again. It was as if they were dead — murdered by the white slave owners. Their babies were left without a mother — and Harriet and her family were powerless to do anything about it.

After that, said Harriet, "Every time I saw a white man, I was afraid of being carried away."

For long after, Harriet's sleep was disturbed by persistent nightmares. She would see horsemen coming and hear the screams of women and children as they were being dragged away. Again and again, she woke up in the middle of the night crying, "Oh, they're comin', they're comin', I must go!"

4

The Turning Point

HARRIET, THIRTEEN YEARS old, was enjoying herself at a corn husking. It was the fall, her favorite time of year. The hot, humid weather of summer was over, but the cold of winter had yet to hit. It was the time of harvesting wheat and corn, a time when slaves from different plantations were allowed to get together. While they worked, they sang and talked with friends they hadn't seen for a while.

Harriet was happily working when she noticed a slave silently slip out of the barn. He belonged to a man named Barrett on another plantation. Unfortunately, the overseer also realized that the slave was missing and set out after him. Harriet followed the overseer.

The overseer caught up to the slave in the village store. Harriet, close behind, waited by the door to see what would happen.

"Slave!" the overseer roared. "Prepare yourself to be whipped as you've never been whipped before!"

The slave darted toward the door.

"Stop him!" the overseer yelled to Harriet as the slave dashed past her out the door.

Harriet didn't hesitate. She moved in front of the door, blocking the exit while the slave fled. The incensed overseer picked up a two-pound weight from the storekeeper's scale and threw it in the direction of the slave. The weight fell short and hit Harriet instead with full force in the forehead. She slumped to the ground.

Bleeding and unconscious, Harriet was brought back to Old Rit and Ben's cabin, where Old Rit once again fought to save her daughter's life. At first it seemed certain Harriet would die. Her skull had been crushed in. For weeks she hardly moved. She seemed to be in a fog, neither talking nor able to recognize her family. Months passed. Under Old Rit's tender care, she improved, but progress was very slow.

From December to March Harriet lay in the cabin. In that time, her master tried to sell her many times. By blocking the doorway and letting the slave escape, Harriet showed a rebellious streak, and after the Nat Turner incident, Master Edward didn't want any rebellious slaves around. But when Master Edward brought potential buyers to look at Harriet, all they saw was a small teenage girl lying weak, coming in and out of consciousness in her parents' cabin. "They said they wouldn't give a sixpence for me," Harriet recalled.

During this time, Harriet talked to God, as she always did "as a man talketh with his friend." Master Edward's attempts to sell her worried her a great deal. She did not want to be separated from the family she loved so much.

"And so," she said, "as I lay so sick on my bed, from Christmas till March, I was always praying for poor old master. 'Pears like I didn't do nothing but pray for old master. 'Oh, Lord, convert old master;' 'Oh, dear Lord, change that man's heart, and make him a Christian.' And all the time he was bringing men to look at me, and they stood there saying what they would give, and what they would take, and all I could say was, 'Oh, Lord, convert old master.'"

Then Harriet heard the news that she and her family had feared the most. She said, "We heard that some of us was going to be sold to go with the chain gang down to the cotton an' rice fields, and they said I was going, an' my brothers, an' sisters.

"Then I changed my prayer," said Harriet, "and I said, 'Lord, if you ain't never going to change that man's heart, kill him, Lord, and take him out of the way, so he won't do no more mischief."

As if in answer to her prayer, Master Edward suddenly fell very sick, and in a short time, he died.

Harriet was horrified that her prayer had been answered in such a way. She felt a tremendous guilt, as if she was somehow responsible for his death.

"Oh, then it 'peared like I would give the world full of silver and gold, if I had it, to bring that poor soul back, I would give *myself*; I would give everything! But he was gone, I couldn't pray for him no more," Harriet said.

But she did pray for herself. "'Pears like, I prayed all the time," she said, "about my work, everywhere; I was talking to the Lord. When I went to the horsetrough to

35

wash my face, and took up the water in my hands, I
said, 'Oh, Lord, wash me, make me clean.' When I
took up the towel to wipe my face and hands, I cried,
'Oh, Lord, for Jesus' sake, wipe away all my sins!'
When I took up the broom and began to sweep, I
groaned, 'Oh, Lord, whatsoever sin there be in my
heart, sweep it out, Lord, clear and clean;' but I can't
pray no more for poor old master.''

Master Edward was dead. There was no changing
that. Almost all slaves dreaded the death of their master
because it often changed their lives. Frequently they
were sold, and families broken up and spread throughout the South.

Finally, Harriet and her family heard that Master
Edward had written in his will that none of the slaves
be sold outside of the state. The heir to Master Edward's
plantation was too young to manage it, so the young
boy's guardian, Dr. Anthony Thompson, a minister
from Bucktown, Maryland, would take control of all the
slaves.

Harriet's head wound was now healed, but the damage to her skull was permanent. It created a pressure
on her brain which caused sudden sleeping spells.
Harriet never knew when one of these spells was coming on. But when it did, she would fall asleep in the
middle of what she was saying or doing. The length of
these sleeping spells varied. Harriet came out of them
after a short period and would continue what she
had been doing or saying as if nothing had happened.

Another result of her injury was that she had vivid
dreams — sometimes they seemed prophetic. She

often dreamt about flying to freedom and seeing lovely ladies dressed in white.

Practical and sensible as she was, Harriet nevertheless put great importance in her dreams.

So, at age fourteen, freedom was becoming a repeated dream — both in her sleep and during her waking moments. This dream enabled her to go on. But the time had not yet come for Harriet to attempt to escape.

When she grew strong enough, Doc Thompson hired her out to John Stewart, a builder. Her father was hired out to the same man as a timber inspector. He also supervised the cutting and hauling of large quantities of timber for the Baltimore shipyards. Ben often received five dollars a day for his work.

Harriet started out doing maid's work inside Stewart's house. But she hated being confined indoors, so after three months of this work, she asked if she could work outside, and Stewart agreed.

Now Harriet worked with her father. She chopped down trees and hauled logs with the strongest of the men. Her own strength increased.

Stewart thought highly of Harriet. He let her hire herself out, and Harriet found jobs on her own and paid Stewart most of the money she received. However, she was able to keep a little of the money for herself — which was more than most slaves could do. At last she saved forty dollars and bought a pair of steers.

Her strength became famous in the area around Bucktown, Maryland. Stewart often had her perform for guests. She was hitched to a large boat which was filled with stones, and she walked up the river's edge, towing the boat behind her.

Harriet stayed with Stewart for six years. It was around this time, at the age of twenty, that she met John Tubman, a free black man who lived nearby.

John Tubman had been born free and had never known the whip of the slave driver. Harriet fell in love with this good-looking, good-natured young man. In 1844, they were married.

Tubman didn't hold a steady job — jobs for free blacks were not always easy to come by in a market dominated by slave labor — but he was able to hunt and fish and keep them in food. Harriet contributed her earnings.

Happy as they were together, Harriet still felt the burden of being a slave. She knew that anytime Doc Thompson needed money, he could sell her. She had developed into a very valuable slave. She could be sold down South and never see John or her family again.

The dreams she had had when her sisters were sold came back. Again, she'd wake up in the night crying, "Oh, they're comin', they're comin', I must go!"

John laughed at her dreams. She wanted him to run away with her. But he was content with the way things were and didn't take her seriously.

"But, John!" Harriet argued. "I could be sold any time and we could be separated!"

"Don't be a fool!" John said, "It won't happen."

But Harriet wasn't so sure. She kept seeing the horsemen coming and hearing the screams of terrified women and children. "And all that time, in my dreams and visions," she said, "I seemed to see a line, and on the other side of that line were green fields, and lovely flowers, and beautiful white ladies, who stretched out their arms to me over the line, but I couldn't reach them nohow. I always fell before I got to the line."

Once again, she tried to talk John into escaping.

"Put it out of your mind," he said, starting to get angry. "If you escape, I'll do everything I can to betray you to your master."

Harriet didn't mention her dreams or her plans to escape to John again. He thought she had forgotten about it. But Harriet hadn't forgotten.

Then, through the slave grapevine, Harriet heard that she and two of her brothers had been sold. Some slave owner from the Deep South had bought them for his plantation.

She began planning. It was now or never to make her escape. Her brothers agreed to come with her. She knew that they couldn't even tell their parents of their plans. Old Rit would be so upset that everyone would know they were leaving. They had to keep it a secret in order to protect themselves and their parents in case they were questioned.

On the evening Harriet was to leave, she walked up to the Big House where her sister Mary worked. She knew she could trust her with the news that she was escaping. But just as Harriet had gotten Mary outside, Doc Thompson came riding up on his horse.

Mary ran back inside. Harriet knew she still had to let someone know somehow she was leaving. She didn't want them to think she had been sold. So she began singing a favorite spiritual for Mary to hear:

When that old chariot comes,
I'm going to leave you,
I'm bound for the promised land.
Friends, I'm going to leave you.

I'm sorry, friends, to leave you,
Farewell! Oh, farewell!
But I'll meet you in the morning,
Farewell! Oh, farewell!

I'll meet you in the morning,
when I reach the promised land;
On the other side of Jordan,
For I'm bound for the promised land.

I'll meet you in the morning,
Safe in the promised land,
On the other side of Jordan,
Bound for the promised land.

She hoped that in the morning when her family and friends realized she was gone, they'd realize her song had been her way of saying good-bye.

That night Harriet set off. She knew her best chance for a successful escape depended on finding the Underground Railroad. So with the precious piece of paper with the names of people who would help her, Harriet, full of faith, took action and started out on her way to the promised land.

5

Freedom at Last!

ONCE HARRIET REACHED Philadelphia, she was safe. But freedom was not all that she had expected.

"I knew of a man," she said, "who was sent to the state prison for twenty-five years. All these years he was always thinking of his home, and counting by years, months, and days, the time till he should be free, and see his family and friends once more. The years roll on, the time of imprisonment is over, the man is free. He leaves the prison gates, he makes his way to his old home, but his old home is not there. The house in which he had dwelt in his childhood had been torn down, and a new one had been put up in its place; his family were gone, their very name was forgotten, there was no one to take him by the hand to welcome him back to life.

"So it was with me," she continued, "I had crossed the line of which I had so long been dreaming. I was free; but there was no one to welcome me to the land of freedom, I was a stranger in a strange land, and my home after all was down in the old cabin quarter, with the old folks, and my brothers and sisters."

The busy city of Philadelphia seemed overwhelming to Harriet. Gaslights lined the sidewalks. People and horse-drawn carriages filled the streets, and they seemed to be moving at a frantic pace — much faster than the slow pace of the plantation. The buildings were tall and close together. To Harriet, people seemed to live and work on top of each other.

She felt out of place with so many sophisticated city people. She was short and muscular. Her forehead still had the broad scar from her head injury. People called her plain, but that was largely because her clothes were crude and her manner so matter-of-fact. The bandana she always wore over her head accented her prominent cheekbones and fiercely determined set of her mouth.

Harriet had to find work and a place to live. By knocking on doors of the city houses, she got work cleaning and cooking. She found a humble and inexpensive place to rent. She enjoyed going door to door seeking jobs because it proved she really was free. She could come and go as she pleased. She soon found a full-time job as a cook and maid in a hotel in Philadelphia.

Harriet quickly adjusted to the size and the pace of the city. It was harder to get used to the loneliness of her new life. She missed her family tremendously. When she thought of them, still in bondage, her heart ached.

"But to this solemn resolution I came," she said, " I was free, and they should be free also. I would make a home for them in the North, and the Lord helping me, I would bring them all here."

Harriet knew that Philadelphia, whose name means "city of brotherly love," was very receptive to runaway slaves. It was the home of many blacks who had been born free, as well as the ex-slaves who, once they reached a free city, stopped running and settled down in their first real home. For seventy-five years, an anti-slavery society had been active in Philadelphia, and by the time Harriet arrived there the city was one of the main centers of the abolitionist movement.

In 1850, shortly after Harriet arrived, she heard of an organization called the Philadelphia Vigilance Committee, a branch of the Underground Railroad. This committee, formed in 1838, was a group of people who helped runaway slaves any way they could. They organized escapes and helped the slaves once they reached freedom. They provided runaways with clothes, a place to rest, food, train tickets, and disguises. For those ex-slaves who wanted to make Philadelphia their home, the Committee helped make the transition to freedom as easy as possible. Because Philadelphia was so close to the borders of slave states and attracted so many runaway slaves, slave hunters prowled the streets hoping to find and kidnap back any wanted runaways. The Committee tried to protect the ex-slaves from being discovered.

The Vigilance Committee subscribed to the *Baltimore Sun*, in which were advertisements for runaway slaves. This alerted the Committee to take special care of those slaves actively being sought.

It was at these committee meetings that Harriet met William Still, a leader of the Underground Railroad. Still was a freeborn black man who ran a successful retail coal business. Two of his brothers had been kidnapped as young children from New Jersey and sold as slaves. One brother died in bondage, and the other, Peter, after forty years managed to find his way to Pennsylvania, leaving his wife and three children in slavery. One of the first people Peter Still unknowingly sought advice from was his own brother, William Still. So William was keenly interested in aiding runaways as much as he could. William Still was the secretary of the Vigilance Committee and recorded the names of every slave who came through their offices, with information about the conditions they had left. This was important because many slaves changed their names once they reached freedom. It helped them avoid discovery, but also made it difficult for any family and friends to find them. William Still later compiled his records into a book, called The Underground Railroad: *A Record of Facts, Authentic Narratives, Letters Narrating the Hardships, Hairbreadth Escapes, and Death Struggles of the Slaves in Their Efforts for Freedom.*

Harriet was a frequent visitor to the Vigilance Committee's offices and became William Still's good friend.

Free and Slave Areas 1854

Key:
- Slave States and Territories
- Free States and Territories

The Underground Railroad had to be clever in order to succeed. Slave Henry Brown is pictured above just prior to being shipped to Philadelphia, where he was set free by Northern abolitionists. Such stratagems were necessary despite the U.S. Constitution's guarantee of "freedom and justice for all." As the map shows, by 1854 over half the country consisted of slave states and territories.

In 1850, Still got word that Harriet's sister Mary
Ann and her family were trying to escape. Harriet's
brother-in-law was a free man, but her sister and the
two children were slaves. According to reports that
reached the Vigilance Committee, they were about to
be sold down South.

William Still was concerned. "We have connections that will get them safely to Baltimore," he told
Harriet, "but we need a guide to get them the rest of
the way."

Without pausing a moment, Harriet said, "I'll lead
them to freedom." It was not a decision she had to
ponder or worry about. She had earlier vowed to
help her family escape. As instinctively as she had
known the right time for her to escape, she knew
now that it was time for her to lead her sister and her
family to freedom. She had saved up enough money,
cleaning and cooking, to finance her journey.

"But you might be caught!" argued Still. "You just
escaped yourself. People might still be looking for
you."

"I will not be caught," Harriet said with complete
faith. And so she left for Maryland. Meanwhile, in
Maryland, her brother-in-law John Bowley had
talked to a Quaker friend to arrange the first part of
the journey. The Quaker was an agent on the Underground Railroad and together they had devised a
plan.

The slave auction at Cambridge, Maryland, had
begun. Mary Ann, Harriet's sister, and her two terrified children were already in the slave pen, await-

ing the moment they would be put on the block and sold.

As soon as the auctioneer went off to lunch, John arrived with a message he handed to the guard. It said a wealthy planter had bought the mother and children, and were to be brought to a nearby inn. The guard did not suspect John might have forged the note — he knew blacks could not write. So John walked off with his wife and children, but instead of taking them to the inn, he took them to a nearby house, where they were hidden. That night they were loaded in a wagon, covered with blankets, and driven to the Chesapeake Bay, where a small boat was waiting. From there, they sailed up the Chesapeake to Baltimore where Harriet was waiting for them. They stayed hidden in the house in Baltimore for several days before Harriet successfully led them on to Philadelphia.

Unfortunately, the Fugitive Slave Law had just been adopted by Northern states. This law stated that runaway slaves who had made it to free states could be returned to their owners if found. So now, runaway slaves, no matter when they had escaped, were no longer safe in the United States.

But while many blacks in the United States were moving to Canada for fear of being returned into slavery, Harriet did not feel threatened. She had faith that her actions would be rewarded and she would remain safe. So, while she sent her sister and her family up to Canada, Harriet remained in the United States, continuing to work and save money for another daring rescue mission to the South.

6

Journey into Danger

BY THE NEXT year, in the spring of 1851, Harriet had saved enough money to make another trip to Maryland. She heard that James, her oldest brother, was desperate to escape to the North. She sent word that she would lead him to safety.

Traveling back into slave territory was extremely dangerous for Harriet. She thought that might be her protection. Few people would suspect that an ex-slave would willingly return to the South. As long as Harriet traveled southward, she knew she was fairly safe, but she knew that getting back to the North would be much more difficult.

One dark night, James and two friends of his snuck out of their cabins and met Harriet in the forest outside their plantation. Harriet began leading them north. But by bad luck, their escape was noticed early. Immediately, James's owner set out with a search party to recapture the runaway slaves.

In horror, the fugitives heard the pursuers behind them. They realized only a miracle could save them from the bloodhounds and the men on horseback hunting them. If they were caught, their punishment would be worse than death: whippings, torture, and being sold to a chain gang to spend the rest of their lives picking cotton.

As they ran for their lives through the woods, Harriet seemed to hear God's voice speaking to her. It said great danger lay ahead. So Harriet veered off to the left. But now their way was blocked by a river. It seemed they were at a dead end. What could they do? There was not a boat or bridge in sight. The waters looked too deep to walk across, and the current appeared much too strong for them to swim to the other side.

Harriet heard the voice tell her to go through the water. She plunged in. Deeper and deeper she went into the freezing water. The water reached up to her armpits. Unbelieving, the men watched in horror. They didn't know what to do. Behind were bloodhounds trailing them, and ahead Harriet risked drowning herself and all of them in a dangerous stream. What a choice! Finally, they plunged in, too, but they kept their eyes on Harriet. If the water covered her head, they could turn back.

"The water never came above my chin," Harriet said later. "When we thought surely we were all going under, it became shallower and shallower, and we came out safe on the other side."

Once on the other shore, they continued running, and finally reached a cabin. When they saw that the occupants were black, too, they approached it. The owners of the cabin, free black people, fed the runaways and dried their clothes. More important, Harriet and her fugitives were able to rest. To thank this family, Harriet gave them the only possessions she could spare: some of her underclothing.

Later she found out that just ahead of them, before they turned off to cross the river, were posters advertising rewards for them, and officers were waiting ready to apprehend them.

By the time Harriet and her fugitives made it to the home of her friend and "conductor" Thomas Garrett, she was so hoarse her voice was nothing more than a croak. And, as Garrett told later, she also suffered from an excruciatingly painful toothache.

Since Harriet had first stayed with Thomas Garrett, on her own escape, she had found out more about him. He was quickly becoming a good friend of hers.

Thomas Garrett, the Quaker who ran the shoe store in Wilmington, Delaware, had a secret room above his shop, where he often harbored runaway slaves. His house was frequently the last stop slaves had to make before crossing into free Pennsylvania. He always gave every slave who stayed with him a pair of shoes. Harriet would later use Garrett's station many times on her trips back with her runaway slaves.

She knew now that Garrett was an outspoken opponent of slavery. He had moved to Wilmington in 1822 and had immediately opened a safe house for runaway slaves. He made it known that he would help any fugitive. He was so clever at hiding and transporting the runaways that although his house was frequently under the surveillance of police and slave owners, he avoided arrest for many years.

But in 1848 he was caught helping two slave children escape. He was forced to sell all of his possessions in order to pay the heavy fine. So, at the age of sixty, he was forced to start his business all over again. The fine, however, did not break his spirit. After his verdict had been announced, Garrett said, "Judge, now that thee hast relieved me of what little I possessed, I will go home and put another story on my house. I want room to accommodate more of God's poor." Garrett then lectured those in the courtroom for more than an hour on the sinfulness of slavery. After he had finished, one of the jurors who had just convicted him ran up to him, grabbed his hand, and begged his forgiveness. Later, when another acquaintance said to him, "I guess you won't help runaways anymore." Garrett retorted, "I wish to say that if anyone knows of a fugitive who wants a shelter, and a friend, send him to Thomas Garrett, and he will befriend him!"

Ironically, Garrett's second start at business was even more successful than his first, and by now, three years later, he was again quite prosperous.

Just as Harriet was an admirer of Garrett, Garrett thought very highly of Harriet. He said, "For in truth

I never met with any person, of any color, who had more confidence in the voice of God, as spoken direct to her soul. She has frequently told me that she talked with God, and he talked with her every day of her life, and she has declared to me that she felt no more fear of being arrested by her former master, or any other person, when in his immediate neighborhood, than she did in the State of New York, or Canada, for she said she ventured only where God sent her, and her faith in the Supreme Power was great."

Besides sheltering Harriet and her fugitives, Garrett also provided her with some money to finance her trips and to help the runaways. Several times Harriet appeared at Garrett's door after having been away for months. One time, when she appeared at his shoe store, Garrett greeted her warmly.

"Harriet, I am glad to see thee!" Garrett said. "I suppose thee wants a pair of new shoes."

"I want more than that," Harriet replied.

Garrett, teasing, said, "I have always been liberal with thee, and wish to be; but I am not rich, and cannot afford to give much."

Harriet didn't bat an eye. "God tells me you have money for me."

"Has God never deceived you?" Garrett asked.

"No!" Harriet replied.

"Well! How much does thee want?" Garrett said.

Harriet thought for a moment and said, "About twenty-four dollars."

Garrett smiled and pulled out some money. He handed her twenty-four dollars which he had received from the anti-slavery society of Edinburgh, Scotland. The group had heard of Harriet's exploits and had sent money for her work.

"Some twelve months after, she called on me again, and said that God told her I had some money for her, but not so much as before," said Garrett. "I had, a few days previous, received the net proceeds of one pound ten shillings from Europe for her. To say the least, there was something remarkable in these facts, whether clairvoyance, or the divine impression on her mind from the source of all power, I cannot tell."

After rescuing her brother and his friends, Harriet's next trip to Maryland was to be a special trip. Harriet wanted to return to her home and convince her husband John to come up to Philadelphia with her.

So, in the fall of 1851, she started off again. When she arrived in Bucktown, she received one of the worst disappointments of her life: her husband had remarried. His new wife was another young slave woman, Caroline, and he was living on her master's plantation with her. It had been only two years since Harriet had left, but John was hers no longer. He would not go back with her.

Crushed but not broken, Harriet decided she would not waste the risk she had taken. She found a group of slaves who wanted to escape, and she led them north with her.

She knew that her mission now was to lead her people to freedom. As she said, "I have heard their groans and sighs, and seen their tears, and I would give every one drop of blood in my veins to free them."

7

"Let My People Go!"

WITH EACH TRIP that Harriet made to Maryland, her reputation among the slaves grew. They talked of her as a heroine and named her " Moses." Like the Biblical Moses, she freed her people from slavery. "Go Down, Moses" was the song she sang outside plantation cabins to alert slaves that she had arrived, ready to lead them.

Her rich, husky voice would sing softly the stirring words she loved so much. The melody was strong and powerful, the message urgent and demanding:

Oh go down, Moses,
Way down in Egypt's land,
Tell old Pharaoh,
Let my people go.

Oh Pharaoh said he would go cross,
Let my people go,
And don't get lost in the wilderness.
Let my people go.

Oh go down, Moses,
Way down in Egypt's land,
Tell old Pharaoh,
Let my people go.

You may hinder me here, but you can't up
there,
Let my people go,
He sits in the Heaven and answers prayer,
Let my people go!

Oh go down, Moses!
Way down in Egypt's land,
Tell old Pharaoh,
Let my people go.

Legends sprang up about this new "Moses." At
first, people thought she was a man. Only a man,
they thought, would be so brave and so strong to
make the trip over and over again, to risk his life
leading slaves to freedom.

This misconception was fine with Harriet. It
meant no one would be looking for her. In time,
though, her real identity became known. And in
March 1857 she was betrayed by a slave named
Thomas Otwell whom she had earlier helped escape
to the North. Otwell returned to the South, with the

devious plan to make some reward money for himself by leading trusting runaways into a Dover, Delaware prison. The slaves managed to escape, and Otwell did not receive any money. It is believed, however, that he told authorities about Harriet. Subsequently, rewards up to the incredible sum of $ 40,000 were offered for her capture. Her likeness and a description of her were plastered everywhere. In fact, she would frequently pay a black man to follow those putting up the posters and tear them down as fast as they were put up.

Other times, when she and her fugitives were hiding in the woods, they'd see patrolers pass by on the road, tacking up advertisements for them.

"And then how we laughed," she said. "*We* was the fools, and *they* was the wise men; but we wasn't fools enough to go down the high road in the broad daylight."

One story Harriet liked to tell about herself is the time she fell asleep on a bench in a Northern railway station. She heard her name spoken and woke up with a start. A man stood in front of her, his eyes looking up at the wall behind her. He was reading out loud an advertisement offering a reward of $ 5,000 for Harriet. Harriet kept her eyes down, her bonnet covering her face. As soon as the man left, she very coolly bought a ticket for a train heading south. She figured that no one would suspect a runaway slave with a price on her head would be going back to the South.

Another time, she was on a train heading north when she heard two white men discussing her possible capture. She noticed them eyeing her, and so quickly pulled out a book and pretended to read. The men knew that "Moses" couldn't read and went on their way. Harriet later laughed about what happened and said, "I was just hoping I didn't have the book upside down!"

Harriet said she always knew when danger was near. "'Pears like my heart go flutter, flutter, and then they may say, 'Peace! Peace!' as much as they likes, I know it's going to be war!"

So Harriet's intuition and her faith in God's guidance gave her the courage she needed to rescue so many others, including children. Young children and small babies often provided a challenge to Harriet. They couldn't be expected to keep quiet when the group was hiding. For this reason, whenever they were in a threatening situation, Harriet gave them a medication to induce sleep. Often she would carry these small children herself when their parents grew weary.

All in all, Harriet made nineteen trips to Maryland and back. Once, after traveling all night in the pouring rain, Harriet left a large group of runaways out in the street and went up to the door of one of her regular station stops. She knew a free black man lived there. She knocked, but an unfamiliar white man answered the door.

"What do you want?" the man asked gruffly.

Stammering, Harriet asked for her friend.

"He was run out of town, for harboring slaves," the strange man told her and closed the door in her face.

Stunned, Harriet backed away. She knew that man would soon realize that her group were runaways, too. Quickly she gathered her slaves and went to the only safe place she knew of nearby — a little island in an overgrown swamp area. She made them lie down where they couldn't be seen — and there they stayed, cold, wet, and hungry. Two twin babies were with this group and were given a sleeping potion to keep them from crying. Harriet had no idea how she was going to get all of them out of there.

"Oh, Lord, you've been with me in six troubles. Don't desert me in the seventh," she prayed. She wasn't afraid. She had faith God would provide.

After a day of hiding, the miserable group glimpsed a man walking slowly on the edge of the swamp. By his clothes, they could see he was a Quaker. He appeared to be talking to himself, but Harriet heard him mumbling, "My wagon stands in the barnyard of the next farm across the way. The horse is in the stable; the harness hangs on a nail." He kept repeating this as he walked.

That night Harriet slipped into the Quaker's stable. Sure enough, the wagon was ready for them, stocked with food and blankets. Harriet collected her runaways and drove them to the next town, where another Quaker would shelter them.

While Harriet always downplayed her courage and hard work, she emphasized her faith in God. She always claimed it wasn't her, it was the Lord. "Jes' so long as he wanted to use me, he would take care of me, an' when he didn't want me no longer, I was ready to go; I always told him, I'm going to hold steady on to you, an' you've got to see me through."

In every crisis she talked to the Lord and seemed to hear clear answers. And she relied on those answers to prompt her into action.

At one point, she started worrying about three of her brothers. Something told her they were in imminent danger. So she had a friend write a letter to a free black, Jacob Jackson, who could read and write. Jackson lived near where her brothers were working.

At that time, letters to all blacks — slaves and free — had to be opened and read at the post office in case secret messages were being passed.

The postal employees could not figure out what this strange letter meant. Puzzled, they called Jackson in to the post office. The letter was signed by Jackson's adopted son who had gone north. At the end of the letter, they read, "Read my letter to the old folks, and give my love to them, and tell my brothers to be always watching unto prayer, and when the good old ship of Zion comes along, to be ready to step on board."

The postal workers knew that William Henry Jackson had no parents or brothers. What did the letter mean? Jacob, however, realized its hidden meaning at once.

"That letter can't be meant for me, no how. I can't make head nor tail of it," Jacob said. When he left the post office, he immediately went to Harriet's brothers and told them "Moses" was going to come for them.

Harriet's timing was perfect. Her brothers had been sold and were to be sent down South the day after Christmas — which was just a short time away.

The day before Christmas, Harriet arrived at the old plantation. Two of her brothers worked for Eliza Ann Brodins in Bucktown, while the third worked on a nearby plantation. Ben and Rit were living forty miles north of Bucktown on a farm that belonged to Doc Thompson, the man who had managed the slaves after Master Edward had died. Somehow Harriet got word to her brothers that they — and any other slave who wished to escape — were to meet her out in the woods by their old plantation on Saturday night. Saturday night was the usual night Harriet picked to start escapes. She knew that the presses that printed up the advertisements for runaway slaves did not run on Sunday. By Monday, she and her group would already have a day's head start over the search parties.

That night, two of Harriet's brothers, Benjamin and Robert, Robert's fiancée Jane, and two other slaves gathered in the woods. But Harriet's brother Henry had not arrived. No one knew what had happened to him. Much as she hated to, Harriet knew she had to leave Henry behind. They couldn't afford to wait. That night she and her group traveled up to the farm where Ben and Old Rit lived and hid in the fodder house where the food for the cattle, horses, and sheep was kept.

The next morning Henry arrived at the fodder house. His wife, it turned out, had gone into labor the night before, and Henry had run to fetch the

61

midwife. His wife knew nothing about his plans to escape. He waited to see the birth of his second son, and then as he started to step out of their cabin to leave at last, his wife, sensing something was wrong, started crying.

"Oh, Henry!" she cried. "I know you're going to leave me. Wherever you go, Henry, don't forget me and the little children . . . ."

Henry knew that if he didn't leave right then, he would be separated from his wife and family anyway when he was sold down South.

"I'll come back for you as soon as I can," he said. "I won't forget. You'll see." Then he dashed out of the door. He knew Harriet and the rest of the group would be up near their parents' home.

Harriet hadn't seen her parents for six years and desperately wanted to talk with them once again. Unfortunately, she was afraid that her mother was too emotional and would not keep their meeting secret. If the truth got out, they could all be captured, and under torture some slaves might reveal information about the Underground Railroad that could endanger the lives of the conductors.

For this reason, Harriet's brothers said nothing to their parents about the escape plan. However, Old Rit had been expecting the boys for Christmas dinner. All year she had been fattening up a pig for the dinner. Having her boys over for Christmas dinner was one of the highlights of her year.

It rained that Christmas day. Peering through the chinks in the boards of the fodder house, Harriet and her brothers watched their parents' cabin. All day long, every few minutes, Old Rit came out of her home and peered down the road to see if her boys were coming. Disappointed, she'd return to her cabin. She looked so sad, Harriet wanted to rush out to comfort her. She knew her mother was worrying that her boys had been sold down South and had left already.

Harriet sent the two men whom her parents didn't know up to her parent's cabin to talk to Ben. Away from Old Rit's hearing, they explained their situation. Ben gathered up some of the Christmas dinner and followed the two men out to the fodder house. But before he entered, he asked them to blindfold him. He didn't want to see his children. Ben had a reputation for truthfulness, and knew when his sons were discovered missing he would be questioned carefully. He wanted to say truthfully that he had not *seen* his children.

He made two more trips to the fodder house that night, bringing more food with him each time. When Harriet and her group had all the food they could carry, and the night was dark, they prepared to leave. But before they did, they crept to their parents' cabin. Peering in the window, they saw their mother sitting by the fire with a pipe in her mouth and her head on her hand. They could tell by the way she rocked back and forth that she was troubled. With sad hearts, they watched her for a few minutes and then they silently headed out to the dark woods.

Ben, blindfolded and guided by his two sons, walked with them for a while. So though he was not able to see his daughter, who had been gone so many years, he was able to talk to her.

The next day, the slaves were missed almost immediately and Old Rit and Ben were questioned.

"Where are your boys?" the master asked Old Rit roughly.

Old Rit grew teary. "Not one of 'em came this Christmas," she said sadly. "I was looking for 'em all day, an' my heart was mos' broke about 'em."

"What about you, Ben?" the master asked. "What do you know about your boys missing?"

Ben shook his head and shrugged. "I hadn't seen one of 'em this Christmas," he said slowly. And the master, knowing that Ben prized his reputation for honesty, figured the Ross boys had escaped without letting their parents know.

Meanwhile, Harriet, her three brothers, one woman, and the two other men made a successful escape to St. Catharines, Canada.

According to a newspaper story written later in Harriet's life, ". . . the first winter was terribly severe for these poor runaways. They earned their bread by chopping wood in the snows of a Canadian forest; they were frostbitten, hungry, and naked. Harriet was their good angel. She kept house for her brothers, and the poor creatures boarded with her. She worked for them, begged for them, prayed for them, with the strange familiarity of communion with God which seems natural to these people, and carried them by the help of God through the hard winter."

In the spring, Harriet returned to Cape May, New Jersey, where she began earning money cooking and working in hotels, and in the autumn of 1852 she returned to Maryland to rescue nine more slaves.

Harriet was becoming a legend. The slaves knew all about her . . . and so did the slave owners. They were becoming increasingly angry that some of their best slaves had vanished, thanks to "Moses." They were constantly on the lookout for her.

But Harriet was also an expert of disguise. Sometimes she'd dress in men's clothing and pass herself off as a man. Other times, she'd imitate an old woman. She didn't need make-up or a different costume. She just bent herself over, pulled down her bonnet, and she was instantly transformed.

One time when she had returned to her old town to rescue some more slaves, she knew she might run into people who might recognize her. She had the foresight to buy two live chickens to carry with her. As she was walking down the road, who should be coming the other way but her old master, Doc Thompson! Quickly, she pulled her bandana over her head. She bent over and pretended to hobble down the road. Her old master stopped to talk to the "old lady," and at that very second, Harriet let the chickens go. Squawking and beating their wings, they ran in opposite directions, creating such a disturbance that Harriet's old master just laughed at the poor old woman's plight. Harriet ran down the road, chasing them. And soon, Doc Thompson was far behind, never knowing that he had just seen his old slave, who was now worth a $ 40,000 reward.

Harriet's successes may have led some people to believe that escaping was easy, but Harriet took great care to plan her trips. Danger and grueling hard work were constant. She and her runaways traveled over mountains, through forests, and across rivers, usually by foot. They were frequently cold, hungry, and tired. And the runaways didn't always have Harriet's fearlessness. They knew very well what would happen to them if they were caught. Of course, if Harriet was caught, her punishment would be far worse than theirs. She would doubtlessly be hanged. Some said she would be burned alive. Yet these possibilities didn't bother Harriet in the least. Most of the time, her passengers trusted her implicitly. They knew her reputation for guiding slaves to freedom. So, even when she'd have one of her sleeping spells in the middle of a harrowing trip, the slaves didn't abandon her and try to make it on their own. Instead, they waited patiently for her to awaken.

However, occasionally one or two slaves panicked in the middle of the trip.

"We can't make it," they cried. "We want to go back. We know we'll be caught."

Then a new side of Harriet emerged. Her face would harden, and from beneath her skirt she'd draw out the pistol she always carried with her. "You go on or you die," she said, pointing the gun at the frightened slave. "Dead slaves tell no tales!" She knew she had to be severe. If she allowed slaves to return home, they would be tortured into revealing information about the Underground Railroad . . . information that could endanger many people's lives.

In all of her trips, Harriet never had one slave return home. Every single one of her passengers made it to freedom. As she herself put it, "On my Underground Railroad, I never ran my train off the track an' I never lost a passenger."

William Still, in his records, wrote, "Harriet was a woman of no pretensions, indeed, a more ordinary specimen of humanity could hardly be found among the most unfortunate-looking farm hands of the South. Yet, in point of courage, shrewdness and disinterested exertions to rescue her fellow men by making personal visitation to Maryland among the slaves, she was without her equal.

"Great fears were entertained for her safety, but she seemed wholly devoid of personal fear. The idea of being captured by slave hunters or slaveholders, seemed never to enter her mind. She was apparently proof against all adversaries. While she thus manifested such utter personal indifference, she was much more watchful with regard to those she was piloting. Half of her time, she had the appearance of one asleep, and would actually sit down by the road-side and go fast asleep when on her errands of mercy through the South."

One passenger Harriet guided was a very tall, very muscular slave named Joe. Joe was an excellent worker and had been hired out to a planter where he worked as the overseer for six years. At last, his original owner sold him to the planter for $ 2,000.

As soon as Joe was his, the planter ordered Joe in for a whipping.

"Master," Joe said, "Haven't I always been faithful to you? Haven't I worked through sun and rain, early in the morning and late at night. Haven't I saved you an overseer by doing his work? Have you anything to complain against me?"

His new master shrugged. "No, Joe," he said, "You're a good worker, all right. But you belong to *me* now. You're *my* slave, and the first lesson my slaves have to learn is that I am master and they belong to me, and are never to resist anything I order them to do. So I always begin by giving them a good licking. Now strip and take it." And with that, he proceeded to whip Joe until his back bled.

Joe said to himself, "This is the first and the last." And he passed the word that when "Moses" came through again, he wanted to go with her.

Shortly after, "Moses" arrived and Joe left. A $ 2,000 reward was offered for him. Rewards for other slaves in the group totaled $ 1,200, while the reward for "Moses" was $ 12,000. Many people eager for that big reward scoured the area for "Moses," Joe, and the rest of the fugitives.

Harriet's group hid in the holes in slaves' cabin floors where sweet potatoes were stored, and search parties passed within a few feet of them. Harriet broke up the group and sent some by boat, some by wagons, some on foot. They made it all the way to Wilmington, Delaware, but police and slave hunters were scouring the city for the slaves. Getting across the long Wilmington bridge and over to the free states would be almost impossible.

Thomas Garrett, Harriet's Quaker friend, devised a plan. He hired two wagons filled with bricklayers to come into Wilmington early one morning. As they crossed the bridge, they sang and shouted and waved to the guards. That night the same wagon, filled with the same bricklayers, headed back across the bridge. This time, however, they were not alone. On the bottom of the wagons were hidden the runaways. They made it to the free states, but now Harriet had to lead them all the way to Canada. In New York City, they stopped at the anti-slavery office. A man there immediately recognized Joe and greeted him, "Well, Joe, I'm glad to see the man who is worth two thousand dollars to his master." The man showed them the wanted poster, which so accurately described Joe that anyone would know him.

At this, Joe's courage totally failed him. He still had three hundred miles to go to Canada. If this stranger could recognize him, anyone could! He lost hope then that he would make it to freedom.

"From that time," Harriet remembered, "Joe was silent. He talked no more. He sang no more. He sat with his head on his hand, an' nobody could 'rouse him, not make him take any interest in anything."

Still, Harriet herded him and the rest of her group on to a train. Finally they approached the suspension bridge which led from New York into Canada. Everyone else in the group was excited at the prospect of freedom looming so close. Eagerly, they all

69

looked out the window at the mighty Niagara Falls
which they were just passing, but no one could
convince Joe to look at it. He just sat with his head
in his hands, knowing that slave catchers would
stop the train before it entered the free country.
Everyone except Joe sang:

I'm on the way to Canada,
That cold and dreary land,
The sad effects of slavery,
I can't no longer stand;
I've served my Master all my days,
Without a dime reward,
And now I'm forced to run away,
To flee the lash, abroad;
Farewell, ole Master, don't think hard of me,
I'm traveling on to Canada, where all the
slaves are free.

The hounds are baying on my track,
Ole Master comes behind,
resolved that he will bring me back,
Before I cross the line;
I'm now embarked for yonder shore,
Where a man's a man by law,
The iron horse will bear me 'er,
To "shake the lion's paw;"
Oh, righteous Father, wilt thou not pity me,
And help me on to Canada, where all the
slaves are free.

Oh I heard Queen Victoria say,

That if we would forsake,
Our native land of slavery,
And come across the lake;
That she was standing on the shore,
With arms extended wide,
To give us all a peaceful home,
Beyond the rolling tide;
Farewell, ole Master, don't think hard of me,
I'm traveling on to Canada, where all the
slaves are free.

Singing, they crossed the line into Canada. "Joe, you've shook the lion's paw!" Harriet told him. They were now out of the United States and in the protection of Britain, "the lion," where slavery was banned by law. Joe didn't know what she meant. "Joe, you're a free man!" Harriet said, shaking him. "Joe, you're free!"

Joe looked up. He couldn't believe it. He raised his hands to the skies and started crying. "Heaven!" he cried, "Heaven!"

Harriet laughed. "Well, you old fool, you! You might at least have looked at Niagara Falls on the way to Heaven."

But Joe had already begun to sing and shout:

Glory to God and Jesus, too,
One more soul got safe.
Glory to God and Jesus, too,
For all these souls got safe.

Everyone took up the song, and soon all of the white people on the train gathered around the weeping, singing Joe. One young woman gave Joe her handkerchief to wipe his eyes. As he did, he said, "Thank the Lord. There's only one more journey for me now, and that's to heaven!" It was an emotional end to a thrilling escape.

After Harriet had succeeded in leading to freedom all of her brothers and sisters who still lived in Maryland, she decided the time had come to bring her parents to freedom as well. She knew this would not be easy because her parents were in their seventies. But in her dreams, she kept having premonitions that they were in trouble, and that now was the time for them to join her.

However, she needed money to finance her trip. She knew that the Lord would provide. Soon after that, she felt certain that a man in New York, a "friend of slaves," had money for her. She told friends she was going to this man's office, "and I ain't going to leave there, and I ain't going to eat or drink, till I get money enough to take me down after the old people."

So she met her friend in his office. He was quite surprised to see her and even more surprised that she wanted money, twenty dollars to be exact.

"Twenty dollars!" the man exclaimed. "Who told you to come here for twenty dollars?"

"The Lord told me, sir."

The man chuckled and shook his head, "Well, I guess the Lord's mistaken this time," he said.

"No, sir. The Lord's never mistaken!" said Harriet firmly. "Anyhow I'm going to sit here till I get it."

Her friend wanted to help, but he sincerely lacked the financial capabilities to do so at the time. So, Harriet sat down in his office and fell asleep, as she frequently did. She stayed in his office all day, sleeping off and on. Whenever she awoke, she repeated that she intended to stay there until she received twenty dollars. Finally, she fell into a deep sleep, and when she awoke from that slumber, she saw that she had sixty dollars in her hands. She was told that her story had aroused the sympathies of various visitors to the office and the sixty dollars was the result of several people making a donation.

In June 1857, Harriet made yet another trip down to Bucktown, Maryland. It had been eight years since she had left her parents. But when she arrived, they acted as if they had been expecting her. Her premonitions had been correct. Her father had been arrested for helping some slaves escape. He was scheduled to be tried the next Monday. Harriet said, "I just removed my father's trial to a higher court and brought him off to Canada."

Her parents were ready to go with Harriet . . . the only problem was how to travel. They were too old to walk very far, especially through woods. So Harriet found an old horse and made a rough cart for her parents to sit in. They set off at night, since they had to go by road. Her parents rode this cart to a nearby train station where Harriet put them on a train bound for Wilmington. Harriet knew that slave hunters would be looking for three slaves, not two, and her face was very well known from all of the posters. She went on the Underground Railroad, and met up with her parents at Thomas Garrett's house in Wilmington.

Before Harriet took them to Canada, she guided them to Philadelphia, where she introduced them to her friend William Still. In his records dated June 1857, he wrote, "These two travelers had nearly reached their three score years and ten under the yoke. Nevertheless they seemed delighted at the idea of going to a free country to enjoy freedom, if only for a short time. Moreover some of their children had escaped in days past, and these they hoped to find. Not many of those thus advanced in years ever succeeded in getting to Canada."

Harriet and her parents joined the rest of the family and other ex-slaves up in St. Catharines. They stayed there for a year. The winter was much more severe than any Old Rit and Ben had experienced in Maryland. Still, they were free! Despite the Fugitive Slave Law the next year Harriet moved them to Auburn, New York. She bought a house with some land around it from William H. Seward, then a senator from New York.

Though this was where Harriet would live for the rest of her life, she still heard the voice of God beckoning her to help others.

8

Fighters for Freedom

IN THE SPRING of 1858, Harriet began having another recurring dream. She was in "a wilderness sort of place, all full of rocks, and bushes." She saw a serpent lift its head among the rocks, and then it became the head of an old man with a long white beard, looking at her, "wishful like, just as if he was going to speak to me," and then two other younger heads came beside him. As Harriet looked at them, many men rushed in and struck down the younger heads, and then struck the head of the old man, still looking at her so "wishful."

Shortly after this, Harriet met John Brown, and she immediately recognized him as the white-bearded old man in her dream. John Brown, a white man in his late fifties, was a passionate abolitionist, as was his father before him and all of his sons. He had conceived of a daring plan, which he felt would lead to the freedom of all slaves.

Harriet met him in St. Catharines, Canada, as he traveled throughout the Northern states and into Canada trying to win people and money for his cause. His plan was to raid plantations and add liberated slaves to his forces. Slaves who didn't want to fight would be sent North via the Underground Railroad. In time, his army would grow so big that the slave-owners would be forced to surrender, thus creating a free state.

Brown had heard of Harriet's great reputation as an abolitionist and courageous Underground Railroad conductor. He knew she had much influence in black commmunities and wanted her to recruit men for his liberation army. He also wanted her to be one of the main guides of his newly freed slaves up north via the Underground Railroad.

Harriet was excited by his plan and by his daring. Brown was equally as thrilled with Harriet. They met again in Boston in the winter of 1858. Brown introduced her to a friend in Boston as ". . . one of the best and bravest persons on this continent — General Tubman, as we call her."

While in Boston, Harriet had to raise money to help pay off part of her house. She returned to Auburn, paid off part of her debt, and then went back to New England.

In July 1859, Brown went down to Harpers Ferry, Virginia, and rented a farm under an assumed name. He used the farm as his military headquarters. The barn became an arsenal, with guns

76

and other weapons hidden there. Harriet and the people she recruited were supposed to meet him at his farm before the first raid.

John Brown's son, John Brown, Jr. , journeyed north to try to find more supporters and more funds. He also wanted to find Harriet to update her on his father's plans, but she was nowhere to be found. John Brown Sr. was getting desperate for men and money. He was getting ready to make his first attack.

Actually, Harriet was in New Bedford, Massachusetts, very ill. Throughout her life, she periodically succumbed to illnesses caused by her old head injury and aggravated by overwork. This time she couldn't get out of bed and spent months recuperating.

At last, Harriet felt strong enough to start on her way to join Brown. On October 16, 1859, Harriet was in New York, her first stop on her trip down south. That day, though, she had one of her premonitions that something was wrong, but she didn't know what. Suddenly she seemed to know that Captain Brown was in trouble, and that she would soon hear bad news from him.

The next day's newspapers told the whole sad story. John Brown and his small group of men captured the U. S. arsenal at Harpers Ferry. He declared he was going to set all blacks in the state free. He and his men then took more than fifty hostages from the town. Soon, though, the Southerners began organizing to stop Brown and his eighteen men. By the next day 200 men surrounded Brown, and that

77

night 500 men had gathered. Even later, federal troops led by Colonel Robert E. Lee, who later became the famous Confederate general during the Civil War, arrived.

In the battle that ensued, two of Brown's sons were killed as well as eight other of Brown's men. Brown and seven others were captured and charged with treason against the state of Virginia, with murder, and with inciting a riot. They were found guilty and would be put to death in one week.

Harriet was devastated. She had put much hope and faith in John Brown and had admired him greatly.

Only later did she realize what her recurring dream meant: It had been an omen of death for Brown and his sons. And it was an omen of death for Brown's ambitious plan.

On the day Brown was hanged, he wrote, "I, John Brown, am now quite certain that the crimes of this guilty land will never be purged away but with blood. I had, as I now think vainly, flattered myself that without very much bloodshed it might be done."

Harriet never forgot what Brown had tried to do. She said, "We Negroes in the South never call him John Brown; we call him our Savior. He died for us."

9

Harriet to the Rescue

IT WAS QUITE by accident that forty-year-old Harriet happened to be in Troy, New York, that April day in 1860. She was heading to Boston, where a large anti-slavery meeting was being held. She had a cousin in Troy, however, and stopped off for a visit. While she was there, she heard that a fugitive slave had been caught and was about to be sent back to his owner in the South.

The slave's name was Charles Nalle. In October 1858, Nalle had escaped from a plantation in Culpepper County, Virginia. He was an octoroon, that is, he was one-eighth black and seven-eighths white. His wife was also an octoroon; she was the daughter of her master. Both Nalle and his wife looked totally white. When Mrs. Nalle's master died, she and her children were set free and forced to leave Virginia. Nalle remained enslaved and was allowed to visit his wife once a year. Nalle's master decided even this was too much, and told Nalle not only could he not see his wife again, but that he had to find a new wife. At this Nalle ran away. He and his family settled in Columbia, Pennsylvania. Nalle then found a job as a coachman for a family in Troy. A man in Troy suspected he was a runaway slave and contacted Nalle's owner. While Nalle was out buying some bread for his new employer, he was recaptured.

Word of Nalle's arrest spread throughout the city. Most of the people in Troy were anti-slavery, and a large crowd of agitated protesters gathered outside the courthouse where Nalle was being kept. All this Harriet learned from her cousin.

Harriet at once resolved to help. Pretending to be an old woman, she pushed her way into the court-room where Nalle was being held. The officials knew the crowd was very excited and so did not bring Nalle down to the waiting wagon below. While they waited, Harriet desperately tried to think of a way Nalle could be rescued.

Seeing some young boys hanging around, she told them to go out into the streets to yell "Fire!" Chaos ensued. Soon the street was filled with frantic people. The officers then decided to bring Nalle down, and pushed past Harriet.

Harriet opened a window and cried down to the waiting crowd, "Here he comes. Take him!" She ran down the stairs, pulled one officer away from Nalle, and locked her strong arms around the bewildered fugitive. She yelled to the crowd, "Drag us out! Drag him to the river! Drown him but don't let them have him!" They were knocked down by the crowd, and in the melee, she took off her sunbonnet and tied it on Nalle's head. The streets were so full of people that only Nalle's bonneted head could be seen. No one could pick him out of the crowd. Nalle's wrists, which were manacled together in handcuffs, were bleeding. Harriet's clothes were ripped and her shoes were almost pulled from her feet, but she wouldn't let go of Nalle. The crowd escorted them to the river. A rowboat carried Nalle across, and Harriet followed in a ferryboat with other supporters.

As they landed on the other side, a policeman noticed the excitement and saw the handcuffs on Nalle. He decided to hold the ex-slave until he could find out why the young man was manacled. The policeman and other officers dragged Nalle up to the third floor of a nearby house. Harriet and some other sympathizers rushed upstairs. The officers fired at them, injuring two men. Harriet and her fellow rescuers rushed over their bodies, burst open the door, and dragged Nalle out. Harriet carried him down the stairs. By chance a man with a horse and wagon rode by and asked what was happening. When he heard the tale, he jumped out of his wagon. "That is a blood horse, drive him till he drops," he cried. With that, an exhausted and bleeding Nalle and a few of his supporters drove off to Schenectady, New York. Nalle subsequently escaped to Canada.

Harriet stayed hidden with some friends after Nalle's escape. She was at risk for aiding an escapee. Thousands of people had witnessed her efforts in helping Nalle. She was every bit as much at risk in being recaptured as a runaway slave herself, and, unlike Nalle, she had a huge reward offered for her. Despite this, Harriet gave no thought to her own danger when she was rescuing Nalle. As always, she was utterly fearless. She simply did what she had to do to correct an injustice. After a couple of days at a friend's house in Troy, Harriet quietly returned home.

Even at home, Harriet was active in the fight for freedom. She made several more trips to Maryland to rescue slaves after her move to Auburn. Because of her reputation for fearlessness in leading her people to freedom, she was continually in demand as a speaker at anti-slavery meetings throughout the Northern states. She told her stories of life as a slave and her exciting tales of escape. She described the injustices of slavery, and she dealt with other issues as well. For instance, this was her opinion on one "solution" to the "problem" of blacks in America — shipping them all back to Africa.

"It's too late to send us back to Africa," she said. "There was once a man who sowed onions and garlic on his land to increase his dairy production. But he soon found the butter was too strong and would not sell. So he decided to sow clover instead. But he discovered the wind had blown the onion and garlic all over his field. Just so, the white people brought us here to do their drudgery and now they're trying to root us out and ship us to Africa. But they can't do it. We're rooted here and they can't pull us up."

In 1854, a black historian who attended an anti-slavery meeting wrote, "All who frequented anti-slavery conventions, lectures, picnics, and fairs, could not fail to have seen a black woman of medium size, upper front teeth gone, smiling countenance, attired in coarse but neat apparel, with an old-fashioned reticule or bag suspended by her side, who, on taking her seat, would at once drop off into a sound sleep."

All of the great abolitionists of the time knew her. One of her good friends was Frederick Douglass, three years older than she and an ex-slave himself. Harriet felt a special affinity toward Douglass because he, too, had been a slave in Maryland. He, too, had been the victim of much cruelty. His father was a white man he never knew, and he only saw his mother a few brief times in his life. He was taken away from his grandparents when he was six and subsequently starved and beaten. He taught himself to read and write, and when he was twenty-one succeeded in escaping. He began reading the abolitionist newspaper, *The Liberator,* published by William Lloyd Garrison and realized that many people felt the same way about slavery as he did. He began speaking at anti-slavery meetings, telling stories of his experiences in slavery, and his fame began to grow. He told audiences, "My back is scarred by the lash — that I could show you. I wish I could make visible the wounds of this system upon my soul."

By the time Harriet became friends with him, Douglass was famous as a speaker and a writer. He set up a printing plant in Rochester, and began writing and editing an anti-slavery newspaper written by blacks. In his first issue in 1847, two years before Harriet escaped from her plantation, he wrote, "The man *struck* is the man to *cry out*. We must be our own representatives — not distinct from, but in connection with our white friends."

Douglass was a conductor on the Underground Railroad, though he said it was "like an attempt to bail out the ocean with a teaspoon." He frequently housed Harriet and her runaways on their way to Canada. Since his home in Rochester was only forty miles from the Canadian border, his house was often the last stop for the slaves before freedom.

The anti-slavery rallies that Harriet spoke at also featured other well-known abolitionists. One of the most famous was William Lloyd Garrison. Garrison, a white man, was a passionate, relentless, and very vocal abolitionist who stirred up much public sentiment against slavery. "I am sorry to disturb anyone," he said, "but the slaveholders have so many friends! I must be the friend of the slaves." He lectured anywhere he could.

An abolitionist newspaper, *The Liberator,* covered many of the anti-slavery meetings, including some at which Harriet spoke. In one issue, it was reported that Harriet "spoke briefly, telling the story of her sufferings as a slave, her escape, and her achievements on the Underground Railroad, in a style of quaint simplicity, which excited the most profound interest in her hearers."

Another writer who made a huge impact in the campaign against slavery was Harriet Beecher Stowe, who wrote the book *Uncle Tom's Cabin.* She based the book on many true incidents and wrote to make the "whole nation feel what an accursed thing is slavery." Her book took the United States — and twenty-two other countries — by storm. Millions of copies were sold. The book was such a powerful statement against slavery that, in some places, just owning the book was grounds for arrest. In fact, on one of Harriet's trips from the South, she and her group of runaways stayed at the house of a free black man in Maryland who later was sentenced to ten years in the state prison just because a copy of *Uncle Tom's Cabin* had been found in his possession.

Uncle Tom's Cabin was adapted for the stage and played all over the country. In New York City alone, four companies performed the show nightly. It was playing in Philadelphia when Harriet was working as a cook in a hotel there. When some of her fellow workers asked her to see it with them, Harriet shook her head.

"No," she said, "I haint got no heart to go and see the sufferings of my people on the stage. I've heard *Uncle Tom's Cabin* read, and I tell you Mrs. Stowe's pen hasn't begun to paint what slavery is as I have seen it in the South. I've seen the real thing, and I don't want to see it on no stage or in no theater."

10

The Civil War

HARRIET WAS DISMAYED when Abraham Lincoln won the Republican party's nomination for president in 1860. She had wanted her good friend and dedicated abolitionist, William Seward, to win. Lincoln had not come out as strongly as Seward against slavery. Instead of calling for an end to all slavery, Lincoln just wanted to stop slavery from spreading to other states.

The Republican party was a fairly new political group. It had been organized in 1854 to stop the spread of slavery. The Democratic party, on the other hand, wanted each state or territory to make its own decision whether or not to allow slavery.

However, as Lincoln said, "A house divided against itself cannot stand. I believe this government cannot endure permanently half-slave and half-free. I do not expect the Union to be dissolved

— I do not expect the house to fall — but I do expect it will cease to be divided. It will become all one thing, or all the other."

Lincoln ran against the Northern Democrats' nominee Stephen Douglas, a man who owned no slaves but who supported slavery. The Southern Democrats wanted an even more staunch supporter of slavery than Douglas and so nominated Kentucky's John Breckenridge. The split in the Democratic party was a blessing to the Republicans — and to the slaves.

In the fall of 1860 Abraham Lincoln was elected president of the United States, winning a majority of states but only 40 percent of the popular vote. Lincoln felt it was his duty to avoid splitting the country in two, and he was willing to make some concessions to slave-owners to do so.

With the country in turmoil over the slave issue, Harriet made her last trip to Maryland late in November, 1860. Despite greater watchfulness on the part of slave owners, she decided to lead to the north Stephen and Maria Ennets and their three children, aged six years, four years, and three months. Along the way, she picked up two more slaves, and they all made their way up to Wilmington.

Her friend Thomas Garrett, who helped the fugitives in Wilmington, wrote to William Still in Philadelphia, "I write to let thee know that Harriet Tubman is again in these parts. She arrived last evening from one of her trips of mercy to God's poor ... I shall be very uneasy about them, till I hear they are safe. There is now much more risk on the road . . . than there has been for several months past, as we find that some poor, worthless wretches are constantly on the look out on two roads, that they cannot well avoid more especially with carriage, yet, as it is Harriet who seems to have had a special angel to guard her on her journey of mercy, I have hope." Harriet delivered all seven of her fugitives to Canada a short time later.

Several weeks after Lincoln was elected, the embittered Southerners set up a new government in the South — the government of the Confederate States of America. First, South Carolina voted to secede from the Union, and Mississippi, Florida, Alabama, Georgia, Louisiana, and Texas soon followed suit.

Lincoln was sworn in on March 4, 1861. On April 4, Confederates attacked Fort Sumter in Charleston, South Carolina, one of the few remaining Federal forts in the South. The Civil War had begun.

The outbreak of the war did not surprise Harriet. She and many other abolitionists had sadly anticipated that the only way the issue of slavery would be resolved was by bloodshed.

The governor of Massachusetts, John A. Andrew, had heard of Harriet's daring exploits in the Underground. He sent for her and asked if she would serve the Union armies as a spy and scout, and if needed, as a nurse.

Harriet, who was forty-two now, did not answer immediately. She was taking care of her parents, and, if she were to leave them on her little farm in

Auburn, who would take care of them? She had spent all of the money she'd earned on her trips down to Maryland.

But she was a woman of action *and* a woman of faith. She had made enough friends in Auburn to feel secure that they would look after her parents. She didn't want to sit on the farm while others were fighting to free her people from bondage. If she could help, she wanted to — adventure was in her blood now.

So in May 1862, she traveled to Beaufort, South Carolina to begin her work. Beaufort, located on Port Royal Island, a coastal island off South Carolina, had been taken by the Union forces on November 7, 1861.

At that time there were 22 million people in the North. The South had approximately 9 million, including 3 to 4 million blacks. With many of the white men in the South going off to war, few whites were left to chase the slaves who wanted to escape. Slaves ran away in large numbers, and many of them headed for the Union camps in the South. However, since Lincoln had not yet declared all slaves free, the Union army didn't really know what to do with all of these runaways who kept arriving in their camps. Because they weren't technically free, they couldn't fight for the Union.

Harriet, and many other people, argued that the slaves should be freed and then allowed to fight for the Union armies. Harriet felt the North was ignoring a vast resource which could help them win the war.

Harriet Tubman is pictured here, at far left, with several of the more than 300 slaves whose escape she assisted. After slavery was abolished by President Abraham Lincoln she continued her work, helping needy former slaves adjust to their newfound freedom.

The great black leader Frederick Douglass felt the same way. He said that the North "fought with their soft white hand, while they kept their black iron hand chained helpless behind them."

As Harriet told an audience in 1861, "They [Northerners] may send the flower of their young men down South, to die of the fever in the summer and the ague in the winter. They may send them one year, two year, three year, till they tire of sending or till they use up the young men. All of no use. God is ahead of Mister Lincoln. God won't let Mister Lincoln beat the South till he do the right thing. Mister Lincoln, he is a great man, and I'm a poor Negro; but this Negro can tell Mister Lincoln how to save the money and the young men. He do it by setting the Negroes free. Suppose there was awful big snake down there on the floor. He bites you. Folks all scared, cause you may die. You send for doctor to cut the bite; but the snake, he rolls up there, and while doctor is doing it, he bites you again. The doctor cut out that bite; but while he's doing it, the snake springs up and bites you again, and so he keeps doing it till you kill him. That's what Mister Lincoln ought to know."

Finally the Union officials decided to call these runaways "contrabands." They were allowed to set up settlements at the Union camps. A hospital was also set up for them. Harriet was one of the nurses who cared for these sick and wounded blacks, in addition to wounded white soldiers. Many blacks had been hiding in the forests, afraid to come to the Union camps and afraid to return to their plantations. These ex-slaves were usually starving, and when they were found had to be treated for malnutrition.

When Harriet wasn't working as a nurse, she advised the hungry and ragged "contraband" how to make a living in the Union camps. The Union troops were willing to let the ex-slaves live near them, but they wouldn't give them food or money. Harriet taught the ex-slaves how to wash and sew and make items that they could sell to the Union army men.

The only pay Harriet ever received for all of her three years' service during the war was $ 200. She gave this money to build a wash house so the ex-slaves could support themselves.

Conditions at the hospitals were primitive. There were many patients and few nurses and doctors. Medicine was in short supply, and sanitary conditions were practically nonexistent.

Disease ran rampant through the makeshift hospital. Dysentery was especially common — and deadly. It raged through the hospitals, killing off one person after another. But Harriet's father had taught her how to make medicines from herbs and tree roots, and Harriet used this knowledge to prepare medicines for the sick men. Her medicines worked where other, more modern ones failed. Smallpox and other deadly fevers also hit these people, but Harriet nursed many of them to health. Her reputation as a great healer grew. Infectious as these illnesses were, Harriet never caught any of them. Harriet said, "I'd go to the hospital, I would, early every morning. I'd get a big chunk of ice, I would, and put it in a basin, and fill it with water; then I'd take a sponge and begin. First man I'd come to, I'd thrash away the flies, and they'd rise, they would, like bees round a hive. Then I'd begin to bathe their wounds, and by the time I bathed off three or four, the fire and heat would have melted the ice and made the water warm, and it would be as red as clear blood. Then I'd go and get more ice, I would, and by the time I got to the next ones, the flies would be round the first ones black and thick as ever."

Because she was serving the army, she was given provisions by the army. However, some of the ex-slaves soon began to resent that she should be fed while they had to feed themselves. So Harriet refused army provisions, and every night after a long day at the hospital, she would make about fifty pies, many pans of gingerbread, and two casks of root beer. She hired some of the runaways to sell these for her throughout the army camp. This was how she fed and clothed herself for the years she was volunteering for the army.

Harriet's next job for the Union army was that of organizing scouts. As the army made its way into the South, its officers needed any information they could get about the Confederates. Were there any troops around? Where? How many? Where were their headquarters? Where were they planning to go? Harriet found ex-slaves who knew the land well. Under her command, they surveyed the immediate area.

However, the black slaves who were still on the plantations were frightened of the white Union army members. The slaves wouldn't tell anything to the soldiers. So it fell to Harriet to try to win the slaves' confidence. She started accompanying boats going up the rivers and into unexplored parts of the South, and she would talk to the slaves as one of them. They trusted her and would tell her all they knew.

At last came the day when President Abraham Lincoln issued the Emancipation Proclamation, ending slavery. It said,

. . . On the first day of January, in the year of our Lord one thousand eight hundred and sixty-three, all persons held as slaves within any State or designated part of a State, the people whereof shall then be in rebellion against the United States, shall be then, thenceforward, and forever free; and the Executive Government of the United States, including the military and naval authority thereof, will recognize and maintain the freedom of such persons, and will do no act or acts to repress such persons, or any of them, in any efforts they may make for their actual freedom . . . And I further declare and make known, that such persons of suitable condition, will be received into the armed service of the United States to garrison forts, positions, stations and other places, and to man vessels of all sorts in said service.

All of the blacks rejoiced at this proclamation. They were free! Curiously enough, Harriet did not seem particularly excited — even though this was what she had dreamed about since she was a little girl, and had risked her life for over and over again.

But three years earlier, when she was a guest in the home of the Rev. Henry Highland Garnet in New York, she had had one of her very vivid dreams about the emancipation of the slaves. When she awoke, the glory of her dream stayed with her and she began singing, "My people are free! My people are free!"

Reverend Garnet shook his head. "Harriet! You've come to torment us before the time; do cease this noise! My grandchildren may see the day of the emancipation of our people, but you and I will never see it."

Harriet, still feeling the ecstasy of her vision, replied with great joy, "I tell you, sir, you'll see it, and you'll see it soon. My people are free! My people are free!"

So, when Lincoln finally issued the proclamation, her friends asked her, "Why aren't you celebrating?"

Harriet smiled and said, "I had *my* jubilee three years ago. I rejoiced all I could then; I can't rejoice no more."

With the emancipation, blacks could legally enlist in the army. Most were eager to do so. They wanted to fight for their freedom. By the end of the war, 180,000 blacks were in the Army and 29,000 in the Navy. Still, equality did not come easily. The government offered black soldiers only seven dollars a month, while white soldiers received twice that. The black soldiers in the Massachusetts 54th Colored Regiment refused to take any pay at all until their salary was equal to the white soldiers. Finally, in June 1864 the government granted blacks equal pay, starting from the time of each soldier's enlistment.

On June 2, 1863, Harriet was asked by General David Hunter to lead an attack up the Combahee River. Colonel James Montgomery led several gunboats. Their objective was to destroy railroads and bridges, to find and take up the mines that the Confederates had placed in the river, and to cut off supplies from the Confederate troops.

The slaves who were working on the plantations heard through the grapevine that "Lincoln's gunboats done come to set us free." And so, in masses, they deserted their work and ran for the boats. The owners and overseers tried to drive them back, but they had little luck. The slaves knew their chance for freedom was at hand. Eight hundred slaves crowded the banks. They left right in the middle of whatever they were doing at the plantation.

"I never saw such a sight," Harriet said, "We laughed, and laughed, and laughed. Here you'd see a woman with a pail on her head, rice a-smoking in it just as she'd taken it from the fire, young one hanging on behind, one hand around her forehead to hold on, other hand digging into the rice-pot, eating with all its might, hold of her dress two or three more; down her back a bag with a pig in it. One woman brought two pigs, a white one and a black one; we took them all on board; named the white pig Beauregard, and the black pig Jeff Davis. Sometimes the women would come with twins hanging round their necks; appears like I never see so many twins in my life; bags on their shoulders, baskets on their heads, and young ones tagging behind, all loaded; pigs squealing, chickens screaming, young ones squalling."

So many slaves wanted to get on the rowboats which would take them to the gunboats that when the rowboats were crowded, the slaves on shore held on to the boats to prevent them from shoving off.

Colonel Montgomery asked Harriet to lead the frantic slaves in a song to calm them. Harriet sang:

Of all the whole creation in the East or in the
    West
The glorious Yankee nation is the greatest and
    the best.
Come along! Come along! Don't be alarmed,
Uncle Sam is rich enough to give you all a farm.

The slaves joined in the singing of this song with such enthusiasm that after each verse, they shouted "Glory! Glory!" and threw up their hands. The rowboats pushed off at that moment, free from the holding hands. All of the slaves were eventually transported to the large gunboats, where everyone was carried safely back to the Union headquarters . . . free at last.

This heroic tale was duly reported on the front pages of many Northern newspapers, with Harriet getting credit for her part.

According to the Boston *Commonwealth*, "Colonel Montgomery and his gallant band of 300 black soldiers, under the guidance of a black woman, dashed into the enemy's country, struck a bold and effective blow, destroying millions of dollars' worth of commissary stores, cotton and lordly dwellings and striking terror into the hearts of rebeldom, brought off near 800 slaves and thousands of dollars' worth of property without losing a man or receiving a scratch."

The article also reported the celebration after the raid: "The colonel was followed by a speech from the black woman who led the raid and under whose inspiration it was originated and conducted . . . many and many times she has penetrated the enemy's lines and discovered their situation and condition and escaped without injury but not without extreme hazard."

The reports from the rebels, though, didn't credit anyone from the North. They blamed the poor command of the Confederate major, saying he hadn't properly drilled his men to act in an emergency. The rebel reports said their troops ". . . retreated without offering resistance or firing a gun allowing a parcel of Negro wretches calling themselves soldiers, with a few degraded whites, to march unmolested, with the incendiary torch, to rob, destroy and burn a large section of the country."

Harriet was proud of her expedition and learned at least one thing during the raid: her clothes were inadequate. Her usual clothes were a dress made of a striped woolen material, headgear made of the same material, and a dark blue coat. In a letter Harriet had dictated to a Northern friend after the raid, she said, "I want a bloomer dress, made of some coarse material to wear on expeditions. In our late expedition up the Combahee River, in coming on board the boat, I was carrying two pigs for a sick woman, who had a child to carry, and the order 'double-quick' was given. I started to run, stepped on my dress, and fell and tore it almost off, so that when I got on board the boat, there was hardly anything left of it but shreds. I made up my mind then I would never wear a long dress on another expedition of the kind, but would have a bloomer as soon as I could get it. So please make this known to the ladies, if you will, for I expect to have use of it very soon, probably before they can get it to me."

She continued, ". . . I have now been absent two years almost, and have just got letters from my friends in Auburn, urging me to come home. My father and mother are old and in feeble health, and need my care and attention. I hope the good people there will not allow them to suffer, and I do not believe they will. But I do not see how I am to leave at present the very important work to be done here."

Harriet continued her "very important work," including a mission behind rebel lines as a spy. Harriet brought back valuable information about where the armies and artillery were located.

Everything didn't always turn out well for Harriet and the Union troops. At a battle at Fort Wagner on July 18, 1863, Harriet witnessed the Union army's devastating loss. She served Colonel Robert Gould Shaw, the white Union commander of the Massachusetts 54th Colored Regiment, his last meal before he was killed in battle. More than 1,500 men were killed that day. One of Frederick Douglass's sons was wounded in that battle. Colonel Shaw was buried with his black soldiers.

Harriet's poetic words described the horrors of the battle: "Then we saw the lightning, and that was the guns; and then we heard the thunder, and that was the big guns; and then we heard the rain falling, and that was the drops of blood falling; and when we came to get in the crops, it was dead men that we reaped."

Harriet returned to her home in Auburn in the spring of 1864. She had been working practically night and day in terrible conditions and needed a break. She wanted a rest, and she wanted to see her elderly parents. Her two years of hard work had finally caught up with her. She was exhausted, weak, and her sleeping spells were becoming more frequent. Once she got home, she collapsed.

After a month, Harriet was able to travel to Boston to meet with her friends and other abolitionists. There she met Sojourner Truth, also an ex-slave and the country's best-known black woman speaker. Sojourner was on her way to visit President Lincoln. But Harriet did not want to meet the president.

Later Harriet said, "I'm sorry now, but I didn't like Lincoln in those days. I used to go see Mrs. Lincoln, but I never wanted to see him. You see we colored people didn't understand then that he was our friend. All we knew was that the first colored troops sent South from

Massachusetts only got seven dollars a month, while the white got fifteen. We didn't like that. But now . . . I'm sorry I didn't go to see Mr. Lincoln.

"It was Sojourner Truth who told me that Mr. Lincoln was our friend. Then she went to see him, and thank him for all he had done for our people. Mr. Lincoln was kind to her, and she had a nice visit with him, but he told her he had done nothing himself; he was only a servant of the country. Yes, I'm sorry now I didn't see Mr. Lincoln and thank him."

Toward the very end of the war, in March 1865, Harriet had recovered enough from her illness to go to Hilton Head and Charleston, South Carolina, to help out again. But before she could go, members of the Sanitary Commission, a group of volunteers who tried to improve hospital conditions, asked her to go to Fortress Monroe, Virginia. The hospitals there were in desperate need of help. Harriet's expertise in nursing and organizing were badly needed. Willing to do whatever she could, Harriet headed for Virginia.

Meanwhile, on April 2, 1865, the Union army took the capital of the Confederacy: Richmond, Virginia. On April 9, General Grant of the Union army accepted the surrender of General Lee. On May 10, the Confederate president, Jefferson Davis, was captured. The war was over — the slaves were free! The United States was once again united.

Harriet was working as a nurse at the Colored Hospital at Fort Monroe when she heard the news that the war was over. Before she had a chance to really celebrate, the sad news of Lincoln's assassination on April 14 reached her.

Harriet didn't go home right away after the war. The hospitals still desperately needed nurses to care for the wounded and sick.

It wasn't until the late summer of 1865 that a weary Harriet packed her belongings to head home to her parents. She was given a pass by an army officer which entitled her to travel at half-fare because she had been a nurse.

She boarded a train bound for New York, and had no sooner settled herself in her seat when a train conductor came by.

"You can't sit there," he said curtly. "Move."

"But I have a pass," said Harriet, showing him her pass, plus several letters of praise written about her by other army officers.

"No blacks are allowed to ride in the cars," the conductor said. "If you want to ride, you have to ride in the baggage car."

Harriet refused to move. She knew she had a right to sit wherever she wanted. After all, hadn't the war just been fought over that very issue? She was free!

But the conductor summoned three men. "Put her in the baggage car," he ordered them.

With great difficulty, the three men pulled the still-strong Harriet from her seat. They hauled her into the baggage car. The war hero rode all the way to her home with the luggage. In her fight with the men, her arm had been hurt quite badly.

Harriet was furious. She had served in the army for most of the war. She had escaped the diseases and bullets that had wounded and killed so many others, only to be injured in peacetime when she was trying to ride in a train car with white people. She realized then that although her people were now legally free, prejudice would still try to keep them less than equal.

11

Growing the Apples of Freedom

HARRIET NEEDED SEVERAL months to recuperate from the injury she had received on the train. That episode made her realize that while Lincoln had declared the slaves free, there remained a long struggle against all of the damage and prejudice the slave system had created.

Harriet's parents, now quite elderly, were both still living with her in Auburn, New York. Before too long, various black people in need came to Harriet's door, asking for food or a warm place to sleep. Ex-slaves who were having a hard time adjusting to freedom, elderly blacks who could no longer work, and black soldiers wounded in the war all came to her. Harriet took in anyone who needed help and let them stay as long as they wanted. To support everyone, she planted a garden and raised fruit and vegetables which she peddled door to door in the area.

One of her neighbors, Mrs. William Tatlock, was among the people to whom Harriet sold fruits and vegetables. Mrs. Tatlock later said, "Harriet, when I knew her in her matriarchal phase, was a magnificent-looking woman, true African, with a broad nose, very black, and of medium height. I used to often sit and listen to her stories when I could get her to tell them. We always gave her something to eat. She preferred butter in her tea to anything else. That was a luxury . . . ."

Harriet continued seeing her abolitionist friends and soliciting money, clothes, and food from them. Anything she received, she gave away. Through her efforts she was able to be the sole support of two schools for freedmen in the South.

In October 1867, Harriet heard other news from the South. Her former husband John Tubman had been murdered by a white man following an argument. His murderer was found not guilty by a jury made up of pro-slavery Democrats. According to one Maryland newspaper, "The Republicans have taught the Democrats much since 1860. They thrashed them into at least a seeming respect for the Union — they educated them up to a tolerance of public schools. They forced them to recognize Negro testimony in their courts. But they haven't got them to the point of convicting a fellow Democrat for killing a Negro. But even that will follow when the Negro is armed with the ballot."

So blacks, while free, still did not have the right to vote. Women were not allowed to vote, either. But besides not being able to vote, another injustice plagued Harriet. Soldiers who had served in the Union army were entitled to a monthly pension. Harriet, who always needed money, applied to the government for it, but she was turned down. The government officials claimed she was not a registered nurse and so was ineligible to receive a pension for that work. Even though she had also worked as a spy and a scout, because she was a woman she could not be classified a soldier. And so, because she didn't fit in any category, she was denied a pension. Various men of great importance pleaded her case. The secretary of state of the United States, her friend William Seward, presented a petition to Congress for Harriet's pension. He wrote, "Harriet Tubman, a colored woman, has been nursing our soldiers during nearly all the war . . . . I have known her long as a noble, high spirit, as true as seldom dwells in the human form. I commend her therefore to your kind attention." Even his petition was denied.

Harriet had mortgaged her house and land before going to war. Now, after the war, she was threatened with foreclosure. At this threat, a schoolteacher, neighbor, and friend of Harriet's, Mrs. Sarah Hopkins Bradford, decided to take matters into her own hands. She had often heard of Harriet's exciting tales — both in the Underground and during the war. She knew of Harriet's immediate need for money. So in 1869 she wrote a biography of Harriet's life, published it, and sold it. The money she received, $1,200, was given to Harriet and enabled her to pay off her mortgage.

In a letter of support for Harriet, Frederick Douglass, the famous black leader, wrote to her:

The difference between us is very marked. Most that I have done and suffered in the service of our cause has been in public, and I have received much encouragement at every step of the way. You, on the other hand, have labored in a private way. I have wrought in the day — you in the night. I have had the applause of the crowd and the satisfaction that comes of being approved by the multitude, while the most that you have done has been witnessed by a few trembling, scarred, and foot-sore bondmen and women, whom you have led out of the house of bondage, and whose heartfelt 'God bless you' has been your only reward. The midnight sky and the silent stars have been the witnesses of your devotion to freedom and of your heroism. Excepting John Brown — of sacred memory — I know of no one who has willingly encountered more perils and hardships to serve our enslaved people than you have. Much that you have done would seem improbable to those who do not know you as I know you. It is to me a great pleasure and a great privilege to bear testimony to your character and your works, and to say to those to whom you may come, that I regard you in every way truthful and trustworthy.

Despite such glowing testimonies and great support from her friends, Harriet's financial woes were never to be over. Whenever she had money, she gave it away. She was always living from day to day. In fact, even while her friends were trying to raise money to help Harriet pay off her house debt, she was enthusiastically trying to raise money for a freedmen's fair.

Sarah Bradford related the time when Harriet asked William Seward to give money to one of her worthy causes.

"Harriet," he said, "you have worked for others long enough. If you would ever ask anything for yourself, I would gladly give it to you, but I will not help you to rob yourself for others any longer."

"In spite of this apparent roughness," said Mrs. Bradford, "We may be sure Harriet did not leave this noble man's house empty-handed."

Mrs. Bradford also told another story about Harriet's reluctance to ask anything for herself. One winter day when the snow was very deep, her father was laid up with rheumatism, and food was hard to come by, Harriet trudged through the snowdrifts into the city. She went to the home of one of her good friends.

When inside her friend's home, she began to pace. After a bit, she said, "Miss Annie?"

"What, Harriet?" her friend said.

Harriet paused, and then said again, "Miss Annie?" Her eyes filled with tears. "Miss Annie, could you lend me a quarter till Monday? I never asked it before."

Of course, Annie lent her the quarter, and that Monday, Harriet trudged back into the city to return the money.

When the book by Mrs. Bradford was written, Harriet's parents were almost one hundred years old. According to Mrs. Bradford, they traveled more than a mile every Sunday to come to church. She wrote, "To be sure, deep slumbers settle down upon them as soon as they are seated, which continue undisturbed till the congregation is dismissed . . . immediately after this they go to class meeting at the Methodist Church. Then they wait for a third service, and after that start out home again."

Harriet opened her house to anyone who needed a place to stay and food to eat. One of these people was a young man named Nelson Davis, whom Harriet had met during the war. He had been a member of the 8th United States Colored Infantry Volunteers and had fought in many battles. However, during the war, he had contracted tuberculosis. He needed someone to look after him, and of course, Harriet opened her home to him. She also opened up her heart. In March 1869, Harriet married Nelson. She was forty-nine and, according to various reports, he was twenty-nine.

The local newspaper reported on the happy event: ". . . Before a large and very select audience, Harriet Tubman . . . took unto herself a husband and made one William Nelson [Nelson Davis] a happy man. Both born slaves, as they grew in years and knowledge recognized the glory of freedom, still later in the eventful struggle they fled from bondage, until finally, by the blessing of Divine Providence, they stood there, last evening, free, and were joined as man and wife. The audience was large, consisting of the friends of the parties and a large number of the first families of the city . . . ."

Nelson worked when he was able as a brickmaker and layer, but mostly they lived a meager existence. Harriet could not and would not get over her habit of giving everything away to the many people less fortunate than herself.

Although Harriet didn't have to campaign to free slaves anymore, she continued to speak at meetings in support of the rights of women and blacks to vote. People who went to some of those meetings reported being very impressed by the small, sturdy black woman. She still suffered from sleeping spells and would go to sleep up on the podium, but everyone patiently waited for her to wake up. When she regained consciousness, she took up exactly where she left off. In her low husky voice, she told stories and excited many people about her new cause.

When Harriet was in her sixties, she spoke at a church in Rochester, New York, with the suffragists, Susan B. Anthony and Elizabeth Cady Stanton. Before she went on stage, she fell asleep. It took the other women some time to wake her and lead her to the podium. When she fully woke up, she wondered why so many white women were gathered. It took her a while to realize what she was supposed to do, but when she did indeed start speaking, the audience was quickly entranced by her stories.

Several years later, Harriet again met with Susan B. Anthony and various other women in Auburn. In a letter, Susan B. Anthony wrote: "This most wonderful woman — Harriet Tubman — is still alive. I saw her but the other day . . . all of us were visiting at the Osbornes, a real love feast of the few that are left, and here came *Harriet Tubman*!"

Even as late as 1911, Harriet was associated with the woman suffragists. A woman who was a suffragist leader in nearby Geneva, New York came to talk to Harriet. "I should like to enroll you as a life member of our Geneva Club," she told Harriet. "Our motto is Lincoln's declaration: 'I go for all sharing the privileges of the government who assist in bearing its burdens, by no means excluding women.' You certainly have assisted in bearing the burdens. Do you really believe that women should vote?"

Harriet softly said, "I suffered enough to believe it."

Harriet's husband Nelson died in 1888. At his death, Harriet finally heard from the United States government. She was told that because she was the widow of a man who had fought in the Civil War, she would get twenty dollars a month for the rest of her life. Even though her own work never was acknowledged by the government, she still was happy to receive the monthly pension.

She had as much need for money as ever. Her work was not done. She saw a tremendous need for a home for old and disabled black people. She claimed it was her last work. "I only pray the Lord will let me live till it is well started," she said, "and then I'm ready to go."

Next to Harriet's house was twenty-five acres with two houses on it. Harriet thought this land would be the perfect place for her Home. She wanted to name it the John Brown Home in honor of her friend who gave up his life for the cause of freedom. So in June 1896, when the land came up for sale, Harriet went to the auction.

"They were all white folks but me there, and there I was like a blackberry in a pail of milk," she said. "I hid down in a corner, and no one knew who was bidding. The man began down pretty low, and I kept going up by fifties. At last I got up to fourteen hundred and fifty, and then others stopped bidding, and the man said, 'All done. Who is the buyer?'"

Harriet then identified herself, to everyone's surprise. They knew her, and knew she had no money. But the bank gave her a loan, and the property was hers. Harriet then had the task of trying to find a way to make her payments. Various civic groups and other organizations held fund-raising events in order to help pay the interest on the mortgage. People from around the world had heard of Harriet's exploits and sent her money. She even received a letter from Queen Victoria of England. The Queen had read the book Sarah Bradford had written and wanted to congratulate Harriet. The Queen also sent Harriet a Diamond Jubilee medal, which celebrated the Queen's reign of sixty years.

In 1903, she gave her house and the twenty-five acres of land to the African Methodist Episcopal

Zion Church of Auburn, to be used as a free home for any blacks who needed it, especially the sick and the poor. She continued to live there, as did one of her brothers whom she helped to escape to Canada many years before.

However, after a short while, the church felt it couldn't afford to run it without charging a $100 fee. Harriet, who had always trusted to God that things would work out, was disgusted by this lack of faith.

She said, "When I give the Home over to Zion Church, what do you suppose they did? Why, they made a rule that nobody should come in without a hundred dollars. Now I wanted to make a rule that nobody could come in unless they had no money. What's the good of a Home if a person who wants to get in has to have money?"

Harriet continued to enjoy traveling. She often made trips to Syracuse, Boston, and Rochester to visit friends. When she went by train, she didn't bother checking the timetables. She just went to the train station and waited for the next train that was headed in that direction.

She also received many visitors at her home in Auburn, including the great black leader, Booker T. Washington.

Church still played an important part in her life. She was a member of the African Methodist Episcopal Zion Church, and often gave inspiring testimonies. "Go Down, Moses," and "The John Brown Song" were two songs she loved to sing.

A friend, Mrs. Emily Hopkins Drake, wrote about Harriet: "We always loved to hear her sing, and I remember vividly how she would rock to and fro, pounding her hands on her knees in time to the rhythm."

In her last testimony in church, Harriet said, "I am nearing the end of my journey; I can hear them bells a-ringing, I can hear the angels singing, I can see the hosts a-marching, I hear someone say: There is one crown left and that is for Old Aunt Harriet and she shall not lose her reward."

Although Harriet suffered from rheumatism in her later years, she continued to see her family, personal friends, and political friends. And, even in her pain, she had a sense of fun. One time, toward the end of her life, Harriet crawled on the ground on her belly as she showed her great grand-niece how she had snuck through enemy lines during the war and avoided detection during her Underground days.

She was bedridden in the last days of her life, but she remained a woman of faith. In March, 1913, she developed pneumonia. She called her friends to her bedside so she could say good-bye to them in person and hear them singing all together. Two ministers were also present. Harriet directed them in a final service. Waving her hand to lead them, they all sang together "Swing Low, Sweet Chariot."

Swing low, sweet chariot,
Coming for to carry me home,
Swing low, sweet chariot,
Coming for to carry me home.

115

On March 10, 1913, Harriet Tubman died and was given a military funeral. In July, the mayor of Auburn led the city in a day of tribute for Harriet, saying that the tribute was not because Harriet was a woman, and not because she was black, "but rather to commemorate the inherent greatness of her character." Booker T. Washington was among the speakers and told the audience that Harriet "brought the two races nearer together, made it possible for the white race to place a higher estimate upon the black race."

To this day, the African Methodist Episcopal Zion Church keeps Harriet's house as a monument to her. There are other types of monuments that celebrate her courage and great works: poems, songs, and an opera have been written about her, and schools have been named after the woman who could not read or write.

The poet Langston Hughes tells how near the end of Harriet's life a reporter from a big New York newspaper came to interview her. As he was leaving, Harriet showed him her orchard and asked, "Do you like apples?"

"Yes," the young reporter said.

"Did you ever plant any apples?"

The reporter shook his head.

"No," said the old woman, "but somebody else planted them. I liked apples when I was young. And I said, 'Someday I'll plant apples myself for other young folks to eat.' And I guess I did."

Says Langston Hughes, "Her apples were the apples of freedom."

Other books you might enjoy reading

1. Du Bois, W. C. *Suppression of the Slave Trade in the United States, 1638-1870.* Corner House, 1970. First published in 1896.

2. Hine, William. *Slavery in the United States.* Viking, 1976.

3. Meltzer, Milton. *All Times, All People: A World History of Slavery.* Harper & Row, 1980.

4. Meltzer, Milton. *In Their Own Words.* Thomas Y. Crowell Co. , 1964.

5. Ortiz, Victoria. *Sojourner Truth.* Harper & Row, 1974.

6. Owen, Leslie. *The Species of Property: Slave Life and Culture in the Old South.* Oxford University Press, 1977.

7. Quarles, Benjamin, ed. *Narrative of the Life of Frederick Douglass, An American Slave, Written by Himself.* Harvard University Press, 1960. First published in 1845.

8. Stampp, Kenneth. *The Peculiar Institution: Slavery in the Ante-Bellum South.* Alfred A. Knopf, 1968.

ABOUT THE AUTHOR

Judy Carlson is a freelance writer and editor with over ten years' experience in educational publishing. She lives with her husband and daughter in Tacoma, Washington.

To Inspire and Capture
the Imagination . . .

GREAT LIVES

BIOGRAPHY SERIES